# THE GOOD MEN PROJECT

REAL STORIES FROM
THE FRONT LINES OF MODERN MANHOOD

A.J. —
CHECK OUT "THE BET"
BY BEN WOODBECK.
THISTLEDEW MEMORIES!
LOVE,
MOM & POPS

A PROJECT OF **THE GOOD MEN FOUNDATION**

# THE GOOD MEN PROJECT

## REAL STORIES FROM THE FRONT LINES OF MODERN MANHOOD

*Edited by*
JAMES HOUGHTON, LARRY BEAN
AND TOM MATLACK

Published by The Good Men Foundation
143 Newbury Street, Sixth Floor
Boston, Massachusetts 02116

Distributed by Greenleaf Book Group LLC

For ordering information or special discounts for bulk purchases, please contact Greenleaf Book Group LLC at PO Box 91869, Austin, TX 78709, 512.891.6100.

Book Design by Poulin + Morris Inc.

Cover Photography by Stephen Sheffield

Interior Photography by Tyla Arabas, Stephen Sheffield, José Zaragoza

Edited by Larry Bean

Library of Congress Cataloging-in-Publication Data is available upon request

ISBN-10: 0-615-35736-9
ISBN-13: 978-0-615-35736-2

Part of the Tree Neutral™ program, which offsets the number of trees consumed in the production and printing of this book by taking proactive steps, such as planting trees in direct proportion to the number of trees used: www.treeneutral.com

TreeNeutral

Printed in the United States of America on acid-free paper

10 11 12 13 14    10 9 8 7 6 5 4 3 2 1

Second Edition

# CONTENTS

## FATHERS

## SONS

# HUSBANDS

# WORKERS

# FOREWORD

JAMES HOUGHTON

IT ALL STARTED A YEAR AGO. I was having lunch with Tom, my friend and former partner and boss, to discuss the memoir he was writing. I had just returned from a year abroad with my family—a year precipitated as much by a long-held dream to introduce our daughters to another culture as by the decision to wind down the venture capital fund we had started nine years earlier. I had enjoyed Tom's draft: The stories of his countercultural childhood and the subsequent turbulence of his personal and professional lives were fascinating. But I could not shake the sense that there was more to the story than the biographical details. While I knew the facts well, something about the telling, about the brutally honest way he described experiences so personal and revealing, evoked both compassion and gratitude. Given that I had been spending a good deal of time thinking about my own story, reflecting on the winding path that had led me abroad and hoping that more perspective on the past would somehow illuminate the way forward, Tom's willingness to share his own journey, despite the vast differences in our stories, provided an inspiring sense of connection and perspective.

By the time we sat down to lunch I had not made much progress on the bigger questions of my own life, but I did think Tom was onto something. Tom's experiences made me think about the stories of other friends—a married friend who grappled with his sexuality, an entrepreneur confronting his son's heroin addiction, and others who, like me, had less dramatic tales to tell but who had faced difficult choices. I admired not only their strength in the face of these challenges but also their willingness to share their fears and anxieties so openly. To someone who was particularly protective of his own story—partly because of my reserved nature, partly because I had convinced myself that my own concerns were less significant given the advantages I was born with—those moments when other men revealed themselves so completely were revelatory. They gave me courage to share more of my own doubts and fears, and in those moments I felt less alone and more connected.

Might there be something meaningful in gathering a diverse group of men to write essays about difficult or challenging times in their lives and what they had learned from those experiences? Though I had nothing but anecdotal evidence to draw upon, it seemed that the men of our generation spend a lot of time struggling to balance the competing interests of achieving professional success and being good husbands and partners and fathers and sons. And unlike women, who are much better socialized to talk about how these same pressures affect them, we tend to keep those burdens to ourselves. While the stereotype of men retreating to their cave is not new, perhaps if a group of men wrote compelling, well-crafted stories about their lives, other men might recognize a little of themselves in those stories and take comfort in their shared humanity.

Fortunately my vague notions of the power of storytelling dovetailed with Tom's passion to explore defining moments in manhood, and thus *The Good Men Project* was born. As exciting as the concept was in theory, it soon became clear that there was a lot more involved in publishing a book than coming up with an interesting idea. With our venture capital background, we probably should have expected this. The past year has been a roller coaster of great promise and dashed expectations, of angst and excitement, of doubts and tremendous personal learning. We have debated the content, the theme, and the title of the book. We endured the rejection of fifty publishers who did not believe men would buy a book of essays written by other men. We have argued about distribution and publicity and Web strategy. But throughout it all I have been sustained by the stories and by the men who wrote them.

I have been overwhelmed by the candor and strength of these essays, whether they came from the early contributors and established authors who were willing to take a chance on an unknown team and an unlikely project, or from our numerous friends and family members who, despite limited writing experience, were willing to share some of their most personal and difficult moments, or from the countless contributors who responded to a national essay contest and from whose ranks we were able to draw some of the book's most compelling essays. Not only does each writer present a moment or experience that resounds (either directly or indirectly) with my own life, but in their breadth and diversity they offer the proof that everyone has a story to tell and that something can be gained from hearing these stories.

The real significance of the project became clear to me at a small reading and discussion group that we organized a few months ago in Cambridge, Massachusetts. To help start the conversation, each person attending was asked to fill out a note card with an answer to the question, "What does it mean to be a good man?" Ironically, I had never been asked that question directly, or even attempted to answer it for myself, but when I went to fill out my own card the answer came easily. Despite the pressure we felt at times to make the book more prescriptive, for it to provide easy answers or definitions, the great lesson I've learned over the past year—from every story, every conversation, every reflection—is that there is no definitive answer. Every story in the book, every submission that we read, has reaffirmed the idea that it is much more about the process than the resolution. My response on the note card was "asking the question."

# INTRODUCTION

TOM MATLACK

ONE OF THE FIRST TIMES I told my story I was in prison, in a facility in Boston used largely for protective custody, to be exact. My talk was to focus on drug and alcohol abuse, but looking out over the crowd of some sixty inmates—including gay prostitutes and pimps who might not survive in the general prison population—I wasn't sure if I could get any words out of my mouth. My heart pounded with fear.

"Hey, Gucci boy," someone in the audience called out, "wanna spend the night?"

I looked down, past my Armani slacks to my loafers, which were indeed Gucci, and then peered off into the distance, avoiding eye contact with any of the inmates, many of whom were now whistling at me. I started by describing a moment when I should have died, when, while hungover and driving along a highway, I flipped the car I was in. I recounted how I had taken wilder and wilder risks and how my risk-taking had paid off in my business dealings, but that all along I knew I was headed for a real crash, one that would destroy my entire life, not just a car.

By the time I told the inmates how I lost it all and had been forced, once and for all, to stare at myself in the mirror, they were silent—no more whistling, no more catcalls; they were listening. I told them I was just a few months into my new life but already things were better. When I finished, several inmates approached me to say how much they appreciated my coming and how sorry they were for what I had gone through. One even gave me a hug.

Lying in bed that night, I felt euphoria at having reached across what seemed an unbridgeable chasm. I didn't expect the inmates to feel compassion for me or to get anything out of my story. But they did. Something had happened as I stammered on about kids and divorce and mistakes made. Despite all our differences in circumstance, my words had affected them, and I felt a lot less alone with my struggles.

Around the same time, 1998, I started a venture capital firm with James Houghton. During the day I built companies with James, but before and after work, as part of my attempt to stay sober, I continued to tell my story and to listen to other men speak the truth about themselves. I came to value the listening more than the telling, whether the story came from a tough guy in Southie or an investment banker in the financial district. In each man's story I heard something I could identify with, and I drew strength from that empathy.

After a decade as venture capitalists, James and I had both burned out. James took off with his family for a year in Paris, and I began writing my memoir. I sent draft after draft to James, which eventually prompted him to suggest that I take classes and also write about other people instead of just myself. Magazine articles about musicians, scientists, and athletes whose stories touched me as heroic followed. By the time James was ready to come home, two things had happened. He had the idea for this book, and he was ready to write down his own story. From that point, *The Good Men Project* fell into place like a set of dominoes. One chance encounter led to another and another. We needed a solid editor, and my favorite writing teacher's husband happens to be a magazine editor, Larry Bean, for whom I wrote several articles before broaching the idea of this book. He was intrigued. It wasn't until Larry met James that they learned they were Harvard classmates—and I realized I would be forever outnumbered. But I also realized then that this book was meant to be.

In my search for contributors to *The Good Men Project*, I went to the three most well-connected people I know: Matt Weiner (a Wesleyan classmate and creator of *Mad Men*), Sebastian Junger (another Wesleyan classmate and author of *The Perfect Storm*), and my hairdresser of seventeen years, Beth Bechard.

I begged Sebastian to write an essay. He was waist deep in his own book, but he put me in touch with photojournalist Michael Kamber. I first tracked down Michael via satellite phone to a bomb shelter somewhere in Baghdad and followed up with him by e-mail while he was in Africa, covering a civil war. I wrote him an e-mail that, I thought, was an eloquent exposition on why manhood is at a crossroads in America. He responded that he agreed with my premise, but that despite all he had lived through and photographed, he had no answers. In fact, precisely because of what he had seen, he didn't feel capable of addressing the topic of manhood, even though it was all he thought about while watching men butcher each other. Michael eventually agreed to contribute an essay, and he directed me to Charlie LeDuff, the Pulitzer Prize–winning journalist who wrote a book called *US Guys* and had just appeared on *The Colbert Report* to give an update on "the status of the American man's balls." I had two cornerstones of the book's foundation.

Matt Weiner, about whom I had written frequently before he became a star, became a fan of *The Good Men Project* and led me to Franklin Reeve, his mentor at Wesleyan, who in turn led me to writer John Sheehy, one of the few men in his family not to spend his work life hundreds of feet underground in Montana's copper mines.

Then there's Beth. She put me in touch with Mark St. Amant, who had written two books, including one about getting married and moving to Italy with his new wife on a whim. Mark became a contributor and introduced me to the people who have formed *The Good Men Project*'s advertising, marketing, and event-planning team.

More contributors arrived through a national essay contest that we sponsored during the spring of 2009. The overwhelming response to the contest confirmed our belief that men across the country have stories to tell.

As the momentum built for our then-unnamed anthology, we struggled to find a title that would fit our aspirations. *The Good Men Project* stuck because we came to view our goal as something much bigger than a book. *The Good Men Project* is really a four-pronged effort to foster a discussion about manhood; it includes the book, for sure, but also the companion documentary film, our Web site, and face-to-face events around the country. Our effort is based on the belief that most men—regardless of whether they are rich or poor, famous or not, black or white, gay or straight, living in the city or in the country—share a commonality in their experiences as fathers, sons, husbands, or workers.

Toward the end of the process of collecting essays from the contributors, I shared some of them with my thirteen-year-old son, Seamus. It made sense to gauge a teenager's reaction, given that the proceeds from the sale of *The Good Men Project* will support organizations that help at-risk boys. We not only want to spark a discussion among men but also play a small part in improving boys' lives by helping them learn about manhood. Seamus's responses convinced me that collectively the contributors of this volume are onto something important. He told me that even the most challenging essays in the book—about war, sex, prison, addiction, death—cover issues that he already has been exposed to and is trying to figure out.

Seamus often has expressed an interest in joining the military. But our conversations never got much past Jason Bourne. I told him to read Michael Kamber's essay and watch Matt Gannon's short film about him. The discussion we had afterward was completely different from previous ones. For the first time we talked about what serving our country at a time of war really means.

In speaking with Seamus I was reminded of what Kamber had said about not having answers. That certainly has been a guiding principle for *The Good Men Project*: There is no definitive way to be "good." When that word refers to a life or a man it is a concept that takes on meaning only gradually, through a kind of soul-searching that is unique to each of us. But we hope that by reading other men's stories and watching them on our documentary film, you can reflect on the arc of your own life and, in the process, begin to form your definition of a good man.

## Samurai Song
*Robert Pinsky*

When I had no roof I made
Audacity my roof. When I had
No supper my eyes dined.

When I had no eyes I listened.
When I had no ears I thought.
When I had no thought I waited.

When I had no father I made
Care my father. When I had
No mother I embraced order.

When I had no friend I made
Quiet my friend. When I had no
Enemy I opposed my body.
When I had no temple I made
My voice my temple. I have
No priest, my tongue is my choir.

When I have no means fortune
Is my means. When I have
Nothing, death will be my fortune.

Need is my tactic, detachment
Is my strategy. When I had
No lover I courted my sleep.

FATHERS

# IOWA BLACK DIRT

PERRY GLASSER

IN JULY AIR thick as soup but clear as cold water, I step hard on a spade's edge and push it into Iowa's rich, black dirt. Setting a tetherball court will be tougher than I had thought.

To dig a hole, you build a hill.

My back reminds me why I have made a life in which I work with my mind. I wipe my face with the red bandanna I have tied at my throat. I am shirtless, thirty-seven, wearing blue running shorts and cheap, nylon running shoes.

Yards from me, on the cracked driveway, I've stacked three bags of concrete mix in a squat pyramid. Now that my back and arms ache with labor, I realize I have purchased enough mix to set the landing strip for an F-14 fighter jet. Sweat burns my eyes. The hole grows to a foot deep and twice as much across. I estimated a cubic yard; now I revise downward. I planned to preset everything into a coffee can but decide that will not be sufficiently stable. Not for Jessica. My kid needs stable.

She is eight years old, and she is coming to live with me; I am terrified.

Perspiration flows in rivulets down my forearms. Once my terry cloth tennis wristlets are saturated, the shovel handle becomes slick. A blister rises on my thumb; another swells across my palm. Prior blisters on my hand were raised by a tennis racket. My hands are the soft hands of a writer who teaches.

I hold the short stub of the tetherball post erect while the concrete base hardens. The post base is actually a short length of pipe. I prop it straight with a few bricks. The next morning, after I set the kit's five-foot pole onto the stubby base, I tie a clothesline rope to the post top and attach the tetherball to the other end of the line. Then I run at the post, hitting it as if it were a tackling dummy. It bends, then springs erect.

In such ways, I make myself ready.

• • • •

The old house I rent is in walking distance from the center of Drake University, where they will pay me to teach creative writing.

Several months ahead of Jessica's arrival, I move in. That February, my heating bill tops $600 because the wind whistles through the brittle windowpanes where caulk long ago dried to powder. But the house teaches me to cook, dust, vacuum, polish, and launder. When I steer a cart through the local market, the spirits of the parents who provided for their kids in the big house guide my arm to Ajax, Clorox, and Pine-Sol—safe, familiar brand names I know from my childhood.

I am told that Iowa's black dirt is the most fertile in the world, and come spring everyone urges me to start a garden. I know less about gardening than I know about farming—and I know nothing about farming. Setting a pole in concrete in this soil from which anything can grow, the soil that nourishes the world, is, for the entire three years I live in Iowa, my sole gesture to agriculture.

. . . .

August 1, I pick up Jessica in southern Wisconsin, where her mother and her mother's husband attend his family's reunion. From Wisconsin we travel to New York City and then to Iowa. When we return to Des Moines, I unlock the door and house air washes over us, soft as angel's breath. We pull our luggage through the door with the unmistakable sense of returning home.

That first evening, after we unpack, buy basic groceries, eat, and walk to the spot where next week Jessica will meet the school bus, we climb the wooden spiral stairs to her room. It is dark. I did not repair the broken light switch; at the ceiling's center is a yellowish bulb with a pull chain. I put clean linen on her familiar bed.

"Before you sleep," I say, "your room needs to be aired out."

So we kneel beside each other on the cedar window seats to open the narrow casement window that faces the street. The catch is shellacked shut. A streetlight beyond the big tree in the front yard casts its light through the lush leaves; shadows flit over our faces. I rap the window frame with my palm until it cracks loose, swings on its side hinges, and then gapes open. Sweet night air washes over us.

"Something flew in the window," Jessica says.

"Don't be silly. Look what a pretty night it is."

"I'm scared." She clutches at my arm.

It annoys me that she sees spooks in darkness. I say, "All right. We'll have some milk and cookies while the room cools, and when we come back, we'll close the window and the shade so there are no shadows. How's that?"

After we dunk a few too many Oreos, I lean against the bathroom door frame as Jessica brushes her teeth. It's awkward for her because she is too short to see the mirror. She'll need a step stool; I suppose there will have to be other fine adjustments. OK, no one thinks of everything. We will become reacquainted. The trip from Wisconsin to New York City and then back to Iowa was good, but to know each other in this new living arrangement we will need to establish domestic routines. In the year we have been separated, despite a December visit, she has grown and changed so much I hardly know her.

"Hold my hand," I say after we climb the stairs to her dark room. We set out to cross the vast, empty space, my arm waving before my face until it finds the string tied to the light's chain. I tug it. Jessica shrieks.

The bat hanging above her bed casts a long shadow across the ceiling.

"Under your blankets. Quick."

Kneeling, her head beneath her pillow, her little behind in the air, she covers herself. Don't bats entangle in girls' hair? Are they rabid? I grab the broom with which we earlier swept and swiped at cobwebs.

The bat is the biggest damn thing I've ever seen. It may as well be fucking Bela Lugosi. I swing, and the bat, using whatever the hell it has for seeing—radar? sonar?— dodges the broom and flutters away. Leather wings soft as Death whisper over my face.

"Stay under!"

I swing and miss again. "You son of a bitch!"

Ahab spat hatred at Moby-Dick. This is no less dramatic than his hunt for the white whale. I bellow profanity. I yell to Jessica to stay covered. Desperate, I whirl around the room, flailing the broom at the air.

And then the broom finds its target.

The bat falls to the floor, where it spasms, broken. I hit it again to be sure it is immobile, and then I press the life from it by leaning all my weight on the broom.

Unspent adrenaline leaves me trembling. I know by how the muscles in my neck and shoulders knot that tomorrow they will be sore.

I bend close. The thing I killed is no larger than my palm, a three-inch mouse with wings, its eyes tiny slits, its frail wings broken. What the hell have I done?

"Come out," I say.

Jessica and I stand over the corpse. I pant as though I've run a mile, and I am covered with as much sweat. Without touching the bat, we manage to slide it onto my tennis racket and carry it to the still-open window. I hurl the creature into the darkness, and I slam shut and latch Jessica's window.

"I told you something flew in," Jessica says and then asks me to look away while she puts on her pajamas. With my back to her, I say something idiotic about bad words and how people use them when they are frightened. When I have tucked the blanket under Jessica's chin, because it is something that I am sure good parents in good places like Iowa do, I try to read her a story. I am planning *Lord of the Rings*, the entire trilogy. Then *Narnia*. Every book. She will have none of it, though, not this night.

"How many bats are in Iowa?"

"I've never seen one before. I think they mostly live in caves."

The next morning, we search for the dead bat, but during the night, something took it. We never find a trace. I keep thinking how small it was, how large it seemed.

• • • •

Jessica and I have been together three days in Iowa when I realize I am inept. She is being noble to spare my feelings. Wrapped in a green towel, her bare shoulders still shining with bathwater, she sits with her back to me. Like her mother, my daughter has hair that falls several inches below her shoulders. I work the brush along the line her part should follow, push the brush to her scalp and tug. My kid tries not to cry out; she does whimper.

It is not courage. Jessica did not have a good year with her mother or her mother's husband, and in her last hope for a place that can be hers, she will not complain to me. Until that moment the hairbrush tangles, I did not realize the degree to which my kid is at some psychological risk. She will endure any amount of pain rather than allow Daddy to think she needs attention. What if Daddy does not want her, either?

I'd planned hot breakfasts against the Iowa winters. I'd stocked up on oatmeal. I'd bought a washer and dryer within days of moving into the house so that Jessica's clothing would be washed spotless. I practiced ironing. Jessica's complexion would be creamy, she'd never, ever, catch cold, and her hair, her glorious hair, would always be lustrous.

But my idylls of perfect parenthood are wrecked by a hairbrush. Knotted about two inches from her scalp above her ear, it rests five inches from the tangled ends of her hair and a light-year from all I had imagined. I recall my mother telling my sister it took a little pain to be beautiful, but pulling Jessica's hair by the roots from her scalp seems too great a price to pay.

I give up and carefully scissor out the brush. Within days, her head resembles a bird's nest in molting season. She looks like a perfectly happy child raised by wolves.

. . . .

Coming from Arizona, Jessica has no cold-weather wardrobe. Shortly after school starts, we go clothes shopping at the mall. I advise any father who waits in the girls' department, whether in Iowa or Irkutsk, not to peer anxiously toward the entrance to the try-on room.

On this afternoon, I shrug off the stares from women who eyeball a man pushing his hand through racks of girls' clothing, but there is no ignoring the mall security cop who politely, but firmly, asks to have a few words with me. "What do you think you are doing?" the guy asks me as he hitches his pants.

I have no idea what is going on. Did I leave my lights on in the parking lot? I tell him I am shopping.

"But you keep staring into the try-on room. What do you hope you'll see?"

Jessica chooses that moment to emerge in salmon pink, size 6X jeans. I ask her to turn around to examine how the seat fits. From the corner of my eye, I see a woman turn away, and it finally dawns on me what this little show of community concern is about. The seat is baggy, but with the onlookers and the guard watching my every move I do not dare grab at my kid's bottom to see how much loose material is there. That innocent gesture might buy me hard time. Because Jessica—despite a head of hair that might be jungle undergrowth—is obviously a happy, clean kid, the guard lets the issue drop. I receive no apology. All this episode means to the biddies who called the cops is that I will be caught red-handed another day.

Weeks before the shopping mall shakedown, I registered Jessica in school. On school's first day, as we walk the tree-lined Des Moines streets, we are joined by dozens of decent-looking kids. Jessica glows. Back with Daddy, she will be attending a new school. Lots of houses on the route prominently display a poster of a blue leaf in a front window or behind the screen that encloses a front porch. A few days later Jessica informs me that these Blue Leaf houses are safe havens. Any kid in trouble or who needs a bathroom can stop there.

Terrific! I call the school to ask if my house can be a Blue Leaf house. Forms arrive in the mail, and I fill them out. A few days later, I am rejected. I am unmarried. "Policy," the police sergeant explains when I call. "Don't take it personally."

· · · ·

Some advantages to being single and a father are less than spiritual. I discover any number of women who take the sight of a happy, well-adjusted daughter to be an indicator that a man probably does not store thumbscrews or a rack in his basement. A bachelor with a happy child vaults to a trust level otherwise unapproachable for weeks. Moreover, an unattached man and a child fulfill a definite fantasy for some younger women, allowing them a little harmless role-playing. I never exploit Jessica in that way, at least not by design; however, the phenomenon is here duly noted.

When I invite an attractive woman to our home for a late-evening dinner, it is because I cannot afford a babysitter or much else. These evenings, however, turn satisfactory for all concerned.

Jessica's nature and our situation require that she meet my friend of the evening before she allows herself to be put to bed. We might read to her. Jessica will insist on a kiss good night, and some young women have their socks charmed off. Maybe more than their socks. Jessica learns discretion at breakfast. She never asks about the other lady, the one who made better scrambled eggs. By the time she is nine, Jessica shares with me her insights about which of my dinner partners has what virtues, and by ten she threatens me with revealing everything unless her allowance is raised. Small bribes exchange hands.

My behavior does not seem to imperil her psychological health. My job is to be the dad; her job is to be the kid. Parts of my life are private; parts of her life are private. She grows confident of my attention's return soon enough.

. . . .

After her first few months in Des Moines, and before she returns to her troubled mother for a visit, I take Jessica to a mall beautician, no appointment necessary. Her hair is worrying me. I expect phone calls from a concerned guidance counselor discreetly asking about neglect.

Jessica lies with her head tilted back over a sink. She wears a checkered blue jumper. I chat with the hairdresser while her long fingers work shampoo into Jessica's hair. After the rinse, I carefully watch her brush it out. She starts at the ends and works the comb toward Jessica's scalp, freeing tangles until she easily and smoothly—and painlessly—can run a comb through the locks' full length.

You start at the ends, dimwit, not the scalp.

"What cream rinse does she use?" the hairdresser asks me.

"What would you recommend?"

In such ways, ever more mysteries are dispelled.

. . . .

Twenty years after departing the heartland, I pass through Des Moines. The city has grown, doubling in size, at least. Corporate America discovered a central location with good golf courses, top-notch public schools, and an educated workforce.

I promised myself I would not, but before I return to Kansas City, I drive to 1327 32nd Street. The gray stucco house still stands. The oak and sycamores still arch over the narrow street, cooling the block with deep shade. I roll down the car window, and fresh, late-spring air rolls in. I recall smoking cigarettes on the narrow front cement steps on July nights, the musty smell of the cut hardwood stacked on the porch, how in winter the frozen logs popped and sizzled when they were in the fire, being housebound after a blizzard, rushing into the street to steal a look at the eerie green sky when sirens sounded a tornado warning.

I crack my car door open, crouch, and skulk—unseen below the windows—up the driveway, pausing only to run my fingertips over the spot on the house's wall where I once scraped a car's fender. It has been repainted, but the scar is still there. At the driveway's end, I confirm what my heart already knows.

In the small backyard's center, near a stand of rhubarb three or four inches taller than the overgrown grass, a pipe protrudes from the earth. I try it with my foot. Solid.

# HERE'S THE BAD NEWS, SON

STEVE ALMOND

I'M IN THE LIBRARY of a small college in Salt Lake City when my cell phone rings. It's my wife calling from our home in Boston. She's just visited her ob-gyn. We've been waiting for the results of various prenatal tests. I walk to the bathroom, lock the door, and flip the phone open.

My wife sounds happy, a little out of breath. "Everything went great. No problems." She pauses. "They did another ultrasound."

By this she means, *I know the gender of the child.* This is a touchy subject, because both of us have been forthright about our desire for female offspring. When my wife told me, two years ago, that our first child was a daughter, I flushed with joy.

"Do you want to know?" my wife asks.

She's in such a buoyant mood. We must be having another girl.

"Sure," I say.

"It's a boy," she says.

I close my eyes. My forehead thuds softly against the mirror over the sink. It's my job now to say something, rather quickly, about how great this is, how excited I am to be having a son, a bouncing baby boy, an heir to carry on our silly family name. But when I open my eyes, the light inside the bathroom is a sickly yellow and my chest is hammering with panic.

• • • •

I'm maybe five years old. This is in the house on Frenchman's Hill, where I grew up. Our cat, Macacheese, has just given birth to a litter of kittens in the backyard. But the kittens came out dead, stillborn in their amniotic shellac. We're not allowed to see them.

The event has me torn up, so I'm inside, sort of curled on my bed.

My older brother Dave appears in the doorway. "Remember when you dropped Macacheese on her head?" he says.

I shake my head.

"That's when the kittens died," he says. "You killed them."

• • • •

Dave and I are fighting in the TV room. It's a boy fight: hurled fists and grunting. Our dad is seated on the piano bench, watching this awkward spectacle. He believes we need to "get our aggression out," and that there's no other way to do it. He's even sort of rooting me on, because Dave is bigger and I need to stand up for myself.

Dave grabs my hair and pulls down until I'm jackknifed at the waist, my head trapped below his chest. "Calm down," he says. "I'm not going to let you up until you quit spazzing out."

"You fucking pulled my hair!"

I'm appealing, I guess, to our dad. But he's no longer in the room.

I finally agree to calm down.

The moment Dave lets me up, I swing for his jaw and land a glancing blow. Later, after we've retreated to our rooms, our father comes to check on me. I'm lying on the blue rug, crying. He tells me Dave has a broken hand, from when he hit the coffee table. He'd been aiming for my skull.

. . . .

I fight with my twin brother, Mike, too, until he hits a growth spurt and becomes too big to tangle with. Our final fight is especially vicious. We grapple and punch and tumble across the bed. We can smell each other—our skin, our breath. The intimacy is disorienting. Not so long ago, the two of us walked to school pressed together at the shoulder. But the prohibitions of boyhood have torn us apart. These days, the only time we touch is when we fight.

Having pummeled each other to exhaustion, we stand face to face. Our chests heave with adrenaline. We're confused, not sure how to bring this to a close. My hand flies up and slaps Mike across the face. It's a loud, clean blow, delivered so quickly neither of us can quite believe it. Mike bursts into tears and runs from the room. I stand, staring down at my hand. My palm stings, but the rest of me feels nothing.

. . . .

Around this time, I become convinced that Peter Guerrero wants to kick my ass. I have no idea how this notion has taken root, but I spend every lunch period obsessing over it. Peter is a pudgy kid with a rash that makes the skin on his arms red and flaky. I am constantly thinking about where he is, where I can and cannot walk, what to say if he approaches me.

This is how I understand masculinity to operate: Either you are a bully or you are bullied. You find a weaker boy to absorb your humiliation, or you are that boy.

A few years later, the bully is a kid named Sean Linden, who organizes a posse of his friends to antagonize me. For months, they call me names and issue threats. Linden never gives any indication of why he has targeted me, and I never ask. All we know is that because I'm too frightened to fight back, I've consented to this arrangement.

The only arena in which I enjoy some measure of physical pride is the soccer field, where I'm small but quick, a star. One year, I lead my team all the way to the city championship game. I score a goal early and assist on a second, which puts us up 2–0 at halftime. Then a teammate tells me that the toughest kid on the other team is going to beat me up after the game. I spend the second half in a silent panic. We lose the game 3–2. I'm convinced my cowardice is to blame.

· · · ·

It's 1981, and Sugar Ray Leonard is fighting Tommy Hearns. It's one of the first fights on pay-per-view, and my father has agreed to buy the telecast. We've moved the TV into the living room because a bunch of friends have come over. There are maybe a dozen of us, men and boys flung across sofas and chairs.

We're all Sugar Ray fans—except for this one kid, Jeff, who worships Hearns. Nobody really knows Jeff. He heard from someone that we bought the fight and begged to come over. In the tenth round, Hearns lands a flurry, and Jeff, who's sitting next to me, throws punches right along with him, wild uppercuts and hooks. I stare at him in disgust. It's such a sloppy display of bloodlust, I think. But a few rounds later, when Sugar Ray is knocking Hearns senseless along the ropes—trying to do serious damage to the man's brain—the rest of us rise from our seats and start throwing our own vicarious haymakers.

· · · ·

I've been at the park, walking our hyperactive Labrador retriever. Dave, my older brother, is a senior in high school now. Mike and I are sophomores. As I approach our house, I can see our mother through the full-length window next to the front door. Her expression is grave, her complexion heading toward ashen. Mike appears behind her. He shoulders past her and out the door. He has the smaller of the serious kitchen knives in his hand.

Mike pounds on the door to the garage. "I'll kill you!" he screams. "I'll fucking kill you!" He's holding the knife as though he's the villain in a slasher film.

"You're crazy," Dave says, from inside the garage. "Calm down, crazy boy!"

This fight began at the dinner table. Mike claimed his right to take over Dave's room after Dave leaves for college. Dave objected. Insults were exchanged. Mike kicked at Dave under the table. Dave picked up a fork and stabbed Mike in the thigh. Mike substantiates this last act by showing me—with great ceremony—four puncture wounds, one for each tine.

• • • •

I work hard in college to convince the world I've outgrown savagery. I quit the soccer team. I rally for nuclear disarmament. I adopt the prevailing feminist spellings ("women" becomes "womyn"). But when my girlfriend makes an offhand joke questioning my manhood, I punch a hole in her bedroom wall.

• • • •

After college, I take a newspaper gig as a rock critic. Most of the shows that come through town are heavy metal. The fans in front are young dudes with radiant hair and bleak prospects. They all drink too much and talk tough. They want to be like the glittering figures onstage— that macho, that powerful. At one of the first shows I cover, a couple of burly guys launch into a pattern of shoving predictive of a fight. Then they start swinging. I leap between the two and shout for them to calm down, but I'm not sure whether I'm trying to break up the fight or trying to put myself into the middle of it.

• • • •

A few years later I'm in Miami Beach, working for another newspaper. I make a right turn onto a main road, and within a few hundred yards a gold sports coupe cuts me off. I honk at the driver because I'm not going to let some dick do that to me. The driver responds by slamming on his brakes so that I'm forced to slam on my brakes. Then he does it again.

When we come to a red light, the guy glares at me in his rearview mirror, and I glare back. Then he gets out of his car—we're in the middle of a busy street—and marches back to my car. He's screaming about how I cut him off, evidently before he cut me off. I roll down my window, meaning to tell him, basically, *Okay, calm down. I apologize.* But before I can say anything, the world swings out of focus, and then I'm staring at my car's grubby carpet beneath the passenger seat, where, curiously, my glasses are lying. It takes a second to dawn on me: I've just been punched. Hard.

The guy hurries back to his car, jumps in, and burns rubber around the corner. Blood is tickling my cheek, from where the rim of my glasses cut into my skin. I pull up at the nearest shop, a pharmacy, and ask if they have ice. The girl at the register stares at me with her mouth open. I am bleeding onto the floor. "This guy sucker punched me," I say. "Right in the middle of traffic. Can you believe that?"

I tell my friends that the cut on my face is from basketball. But I know the truth. I'm lucky the guy didn't drag me out of my car, didn't have a weapon, didn't turn me into the sort of violent headline I might read about in the Metro section while imagining the victim as a pathetic wimp.

• • • •

For the next decade there's always some guy I feel I should fight. The guy who throws elbows in our pickup hoops game at Flamingo Park. The guy who spends months baiting me in grad school. The guy who sells me a bag of fake pot and refuses to refund my money. I sit around for hours at a time, reliving our confrontations, wishing I had the courage to punch these dudes in the face.

• • • •

It's tempting to blame all this on my father. That would be the safe move. Perhaps if he'd encouraged us to share our feelings rather than pummel each other, my brothers and I would have entered the world without fear and loathing. We would have become secure citizens, ready to talk things through. But that would miss the point, that masculinity has always been governed by aggression.

To put it more starkly: Aggression is the means by which boys learn to share their feelings. Not even the most loving father can protect his son from the playgrounds, the bars and parking lots where bullies lurk, where soft emotions are hunted down and targeted, where fear becomes rage, and rage becomes violence.

. . . .

My wife is downstairs with our daughter. I can hear them playing with the new paint set. I'm upstairs working on my novel. Except half the time, I'm not writing at all. I'm trolling YouTube for old boxing matches, street brawls, ultimate fighting—the pornography of the bullied. I watch these scenes with a scalding, masturbatory shame. My fists twitch and flex. I'm like a Catholic kid frisking myself for that forbidden rush of adrenaline.

. . . .

Or maybe I'm in my car, immersed in the molten wrath of Boston traffic. This is where I indulge my other secret vice: talk radio. Limbaugh, Hannity, Savage—our maestros of rage, each a Joe McCarthy Mini-Me. Grievance is their siren's call. "You are all victims!" they sing. "Are you going to let these [fill in the blank] kick us around? Fight back!"

These guys represent everything I despise. They're vampires of the soul, feeding on the psychic damage of their congregations. And yet listening to them is a kind of seduction. It's like tuning in to an emotional oldies station. The louder they wail, the deeper I descend into that primordial realm where nobody ever admits he's wrong or uncertain or frightened, where sadism is the chosen means of eradicating shame. Welcome to masculinity stunted at age five.

. . . .

And whom does history commemorate if not those men most effective at marshaling their aggression to shape the world? For every Gandhi, a hundred Hitlers. For every Enlightenment, a hundred Inquisitions. For every treaty, a hundred wars.

What I'm asking here is, Do we ever outgrow our savagery? Is there any way to strip from us the masculine pathologies acquired over millions of years of evolution?

Let me put all this in a more personal light: How am I to protect my son from a world that lives inside of me?

I have plenty of fancy ideas about how this might happen, about what it means to be a good man, and I've spent many years trying to publicize my own glowing empathy. But the truth is I remain a prisoner of terror and rage, one minute puffing out my chest, the next cowering, dreaming of a power that resides in valor, in the ability to inflict physical harm. It's horrible who I am.

. . . .

So now you know why I feared having a son, and why, when I gaze down at my newborn boy sleeping—he is three days old as I write this—I am sometimes filled with dread. I offer no happy ending here, no eleventh-hour homily about the rescuing powers of forgiveness. A quick look at the state of the world should dispel such mush. All I can say is that I'll do my best with the love I have. I'll hope my boy becomes someone different from his father, braver in the right ways, less frightened. This, it seems to me, is the only reasonable hope fathers can offer their sons.

# NO ONE SAW A THING

JEFFREY K. WALLACE

THERE'S ALWAYS ONE KID in the neighborhood everybody loves to torment; in Windsor Heights it was me. My short list of therapy-inducing childhood memories includes being stuffed into a sleeping bag and tied to a tree branch, being locked in a garage and pelted with bottle rockets, and being excluded from everything potentially fun, competitive, or criminal. I would laugh about it later, of course, when I managed to reach adulthood.

But now I have a son. His name is Aaron. The first blow hit him right in the freckles. I didn't give him a brother and he never had many enemies, or friends, so it was his first fist to the face—and it landed right where his mother kisses him at bedtime. That first punch, like a first kiss, sort of, without the spit, is something a guy never forgets.

The second blow knocked him off the curb and into the street. His backpack, a fifteen-pound pile of hardcovers he carried but never read, slid down off his shoulders and pinned his wrists to his sides. One of the boys planted a Nike: Aaron skidded out onto the asphalt, his shirt collecting all the grit and gravel within a spit-wad's reach of our driveway, barely thirty feet from our front door.

No one saw a thing; I called around to ask.

In my mind's eye I can see Aaron smiling as he's falling, and he's wearing one of those silly little grins—he was always smiling at the wrong times. It never occurred to me to tell a nine-year-old not to grin if he was getting his tail kicked.

· · · ·

It was late afternoon when Katherine met me at the door with details and evidence in hand. Parenthood has a way of repeatedly pulling this kind of thing on you. Won't there ever come a day when I see it coming? Maybe a red flag in the yard, so I know to keep on driving?

I examined his pants with the dirty shoe prints and a street-scuffed shirt with a heel mark, while Aaron stood, shifting from foot to foot, chewing his T-shirt. A dark saliva stain the size of a softball fanned out from the hem.

"Show your father your face," Katherine said. "Show him your face, Aaron."

Aaron stood before me. I couldn't help but smile at first—until I saw the welt beneath his eye. "Oh no," I said, lifting a finger to touch it. He wouldn't let me. "Was the kid who hit you wearing a ring?"

He popped the wet cotton from his lips. "Duh," he said.

I'd spent half my life dreaming about things that never happen. But this? I grabbed my boy and squeezed—his spindly body, smooth arms, elementary-school aroma—and just like that got caught up in something. No doubt there's a name for it somewhere in some parenting textbook I never read, a name that captures the notion that there's a reservoir filled with everything we've ever held back, and that it can rise up and splash without warning.

"Let go of me," he said.

I didn't want to. Cross-examination time. "Do you know these boys?"

"No."

"Are they from your school?"

He nodded.

"Did you run into them on the playground or bump them or say something or . . ."

No, no, and no. He'd done *nothing*. I believed him. They'd followed him home from school and pounced.

"Man," I muttered, flashing back decades to the angry face of Danny Murphy, the kid who chased me around a parked car screaming that he wanted to pound my face in. What had I done? Nothing! Not a *thing*! "We're going to do something about this, Aaron. *I'm* going to do something," I told him. "What they did was *wrong*."

He looked at me and nodded.

"I'm going to stand up for you," I said.

Why didn't my old man ever say that for me?

Aaron provided a thin description of the perpetrators—shirt and hair colors, tennis shoes—and we set off on a bully hunt. It didn't take long to spot one, and when I pulled up to the curb, just a block from our house, he took off. I threw the car in park and opened my door. A man in a nearby driveway stood hosing his cement. I went to him and asked if he knew where that boy lived.

He squirted a shot of water into his next-door neighbors' yard. "Right there," he said. "Joshua."

I asked for the family's name. He didn't seem embarrassed about not remembering it: "We don't get along that well."

When I got back in the car I had more than a fleeting notion to tell Aaron I'd taken care of everything. Part of me wanted to lie and wish it all away, to tell him I'd just talked to one of the boys' dads and that everything was taken care of. I yanked the keys from the ignition. "I know where one of them lives," I sighed. "Come on."

. . . .

Joshua Templar's mother was preparing for a party, and in spite of the fact that she'd never seen me before, she opened her door wide enough for me to get a good look inside. Her living room was decked out with balloons and candles, and a table next to the baby grand piano was covered with silver-wrapped boxes. A dozen framed photos of smiling, well-dressed people lined the tabletops.

I introduced myself with a handshake—Who knew pressing the flesh was involved in getting to the bottom of such things?—and told her where I lived. Then I introduced Aaron and told her my son had been "roughed up" on his way home from school. She gasped, naturally; one of those "In this neighborhood?" reactions. Aaron stood silently at my side, chewing the bottom hem of his shirt.

It wasn't until I described the perpetrator's hair and shirt color that the woman's hand snapped up to her mouth. *"Joshua?"* she asked.

"I don't know. But the one who punched his face wears a ring. You can still see the imprint on his cheek." I pointed at my boy.

She leaned in for a look, and her lips moved. Her eyes welled.

I looked at Aaron, who looked at me. We both looked away and out toward the man still hosing his driveway. He gave us a thumbs-up.

As Joshua's mother apologized, Aaron grew fidgety. He just wanted to see someone get whacked, or so I figured. Or maybe it was me.

Joshua, meanwhile, was nowhere to be found. I gave his mother my phone number, and we left with her promise that she'd call us when she got her hands on her son.

Forty minutes later we were back on the doorstep, but this time I was nervous. I'd had time to fantasize about outcomes. Was Joshua's father going to be there too? Aaron was especially twitchy.

"We have to do this," I told him. "We *have* to. I know it's hard, but . . ." I have six thousand clichés and speeches awaiting delivery, yet not one of them focuses on what to say or do when your kid gets beaten up without provocation.

The boy described as "white hair, red shirt" came out of the house with his head down. His mother pointed to a step; he sat. She made it clear to us that Joshua was in trouble of "the most serious kind, I can assure you." He had admitted that he and a friend had lashed out at Aaron after school.

"Why?" I asked. "Why did you hit him?"

Joshua shrugged.

"Did Aaron say something he shouldn't have?"

He shrugged some more.

"Is he in your class at school?" his mother asked. I already knew the answer to that one: Joshua was a year older. So was the other kid. Still, Joshua said nothing, no matter what was asked or who asked it. For a kid with such a loose temper, he sure had an economy with words.

"I'll tell you what, Joshua," I said, "I want you two to stay away from each other. At school, around here—anywhere. Understand? If you see each other, then ignore each other. Just keep away. Got it?" A little voice inside my head cheered *Go, Dad! You're the man!* I'd tracked down a bully. I'd faced a fear. I'd shown my son what it meant to identify a problem and take action to fix it. This was going to go down in family lore as one of my shining moments. I'd make sure of it. Okay, I thought, so Aaron took a punch. Life's not fair, right? Maybe now he'll be more wary, more streetwise. That would be good.

With a vision of my wife's proud face flashing through my mind, I bid good-bye and was one step toward the street when Joshua's head snapped up, and he growled in a voice that would have sent me running if he'd had scissors.

"He *sniffed* me!" the boy shouted. "That's why I hit him!"

I turned around. "He what?"

"He was sniffing me! He was sniffing *all* of us, at recess. He wouldn't leave us alone!"

"He was *sniffing* you? What do you mean he was sniffing you?" His mother crossed her arms fast and tight.

Joshua snorted his wrist. "Like that!" he said. He snarled and thrust a ringed finger at Aaron. "I *told him* to stop and he *wouldn't!* It's embarrassing!"

We all turned to Aaron. He squeezed his eyes shut.

"That's still no reason to . . ." I began.

"So we followed him. And when we came up to him he put his arms out and said, 'Group hug!' "

Aaron's teeth clenched so tight his lips went white at the edges.

"He's *weird!*" Joshua screamed. "Group hug? *That's* why I hit him!

'Cause he's so *weird!*"

Joshua buried his head in his knees and began to cry.

"Aaron!" I growled. "Did you . . . Did . . . ? *Aaron!*"

No matter what I said—and I'm not sure of everything I said or tried to say in those next few moments—my son would not speak. He'd jacked his shoulders up so high they had glued themselves to his earlobes. He wouldn't even open his eyes, not when I put my hand on his shoulder—gently—not when I asked him to "Look at me," and not when I commanded him to "Say something!"

Everything suddenly looked different, my boy in particular. "You *sniffed* him?!"

Our secret was out.

Aaron had been sniffing things around the house for a long, long time—sniffing our clothing, his toys, the doorknobs, the cat, the furniture—and chewing things too, mainly his T-shirts. And towels. And the curtains. Pretty much any piece of cloth that hangs. These were problems we hadn't solved yet. That's how I looked at it. A handful of strange little habits. Things he'd grow out of. Private, harmless, around-the-house quirks.

There now were just three of us accessible for conversation; Aaron had shut down, and I knew him well enough to know that once he'd shut down there was no turning him on again. I offered a brief apology—it was my fault, I said, my fault, no explanation—and steered my son toward the car.

· · · ·

The child psychiatrist came highly recommended. She was a "prodigy" in the field—that's one of the things she mentioned in our first meeting. "I am the best," she said, clasping her paperweight and leaning toward us over the desk. "I will help you. I see children like Aaron every day."

We told her the "roughed up" story.

"If you had only brought him to see me a couple of years ago," she grinned, "I could have prevented this kind of thing."

Katherine hated her instantly. I, on the other hand, was curious. But my curiosity lasted until our second meeting, when, after spending forty minutes in private working with our son, she told us, "Why do you call this boy quirky? He is not quirky. He is autistic."

Katherine grabbed the tissues. I bowed my head and closed my eyes. Red flags everywhere. Why hadn't I seen them? Where had I been looking?

. . . .

Flash forward. Several months have passed, and the neighborhood feels safe again. Things are looking up. Aaron no longer walks home from school, for one thing. We drive him—to and from a smaller school with teachers who understand how to work with a variety of social and processing styles. I no longer dismiss him as "quirky," either. Thanks to a team of agreeable physicians who see lots of boys like Aaron—we dumped the prodigy—I understand that the autism spectrum is a broad one, and Katherine and I have spent days and nights learning all we can about what it means to have a son at the "high-functioning" end of it. Best of all, Aaron is thriving in a school setting for the first time in his life, and he's no longer the only kid he knows who can't stand hot dogs or hamburgers or fish or beans or rice or anything green or crusty or not folded or cut into triangles. He's making friends. And having fun.

When his new school recently held a Friday morning doughnut-centered social activity for fathers and sons, we showed up early. Aaron grabbed a chocolate long john and planted himself on my lap. Small talk isn't our thing, so we just sat and enjoyed the scenery. Every so often I'd reach up and squeeze his shoulder or rub his back, or ask him how many doughnuts he'd eaten. Four.

When it was time for me to go, I stood up once again. Aaron said, "Bye," and I brushed a bit of chocolate from his face, from a nice tender spot just below a field of freckles. The skin there is still soft and as smooth as frosting. A minute later he was off to class, and I stepped outside into the California winter sun.

Out of the blue, all of the changes that had altered our lives in the last couple of months—all the worrying and wondering and retooling of expectations, all the appointments and arguments, all the *everything*—came to a head. I was walking down the sidewalk when my eyes welled up and my chest heaved. I grabbed for a breath—it was that secret reservoir again, way closer to the surface than I imagined—and there were people heading my way. I made a point of looking up into the sun as I passed them. Looking into the sun brings tears sometimes. I didn't really let go until I got into my car.

# BLINDFOLDED

## JOHN OLIVER

OUR DAUGHTER KATE was conceived within minutes of my get-ting home from Iraq. I was a young lieutenant in the 82nd Airborne Division, and I'd married Melissa just a few weeks before my unit's unexpected deployment to the Persian Gulf. In Iraq, I had done what most frightened men do during war: I thought about the rest of my life. I repeatedly tried to make a list of the things that I wanted to accomplish with my remaining years, but I couldn't finish it, because I couldn't think past my immediate fears over whether I would survive the next few months.

Why are there baby booms after wars? The answer is obvious to me. They're not the products of pent-up sexual energy, although that undoubtedly is a factor. The real cause is human nature: When we confront our mortality, we're driven to reproduce. It's primal, it's instinctive, and it's a powerful force. The only thing I knew I wanted was to make it home and become a father.

I adored Kate. She was a wild and amazing girl. I remember the evening that Kate and I went for a walk in the neighborhood and she discovered her shadow. She had just mastered walking, and her brain was exploding with language. We were toddling along together and Kate was looking at, pointing at, and shouting at everything she saw, ecstatic with her surroundings. But when she looked down at the street and saw the grayish shape that looked like her reflection and moved whenever she did, she became entranced and speechless.

There was another night when we had dinner at a friend's house, next to the eighteenth fairway of a golf course. After dinner we wandered over to the driving range to hit a few balls. We brought Kate's big plastic golf clubs and balls, but when we got to the tee she wanted no part of those kids' toys. She grabbed a full-size driver and screamed wildly as she clobbered the striped range balls right out of the bucket.

At home, Kate loved to take a clean sock from the laundry basket and put it over her eyes like a blindfold. She would tilt her head back so the sock wouldn't fall off, and then she would run around the house with her eyes covered, unable to see where she was going, howling with excitement. Melissa, my wife, and I were terrified that Kate might crash into the brick hearth or bump her head somewhere and need stitches. But her recklessness was inspiring and instructive to us as parents. It spoke of the unknown and of making peace with the limitations of our control.

. . . .

A few weeks before Kate became sick I went to a soldier's funeral. I didn't know the man, though we had served in the same unit. A couple of my buddies were going to the funeral, so I saw it as an excuse to go out with the boys; in my experience, funerals always involved some drinking.

On the way to the funeral I learned that the soldier had killed himself. His wife had asked him for a divorce only days before, and he'd shot himself in the heart. I thought it was a poetic thing to do.

When I met the widow in the receiving line at the funeral home, I didn't think she looked like a woman worth killing yourself over. I muttered the detached phrase, "I'm sorry for your loss." Then she seemed to lean forward to kiss my cheek, and I recoiled. She said, "Thank you." Then I grabbed my two buddies so that we could leave and get a drink.

At the bar, we had a few rounds of beer, and at some point the subject of golf came up. I was a horrible golfer—still am—but I assured my two buddies that if I invested enough time in the game I could one day be a pro. They both had seen me play golf and knew my confidence was misplaced.

My friend Kevin tried to explain to me that there are, in fact, some things that are beyond our control, and that he was pretty sure it wasn't within my ability to become a professional golfer. I dismissed his remark as heresy. Kevin was speaking from experience: He had been dropped from Ranger school—something he was constantly reminded of by his peers with a Ranger tab on their uniforms—and his marriage was in trouble. He continued to try reasoning with me, telling me a story about his father's business, how it was destroyed by a partner who embezzled funds, and how his father had failed despite his virtues. But the message was lost on me, and we returned to our beers.

. . . .

Kate was eighteen months old and never before had been sick. She had a runny nose for a few days but no other symptoms. Then one evening she developed a high fever. As a precaution we took her to Womack Army Hospital at Fort Bragg that night. The waiting room was filled with dozens of soldiers who had been injured during the athletic competitions held as part of All-American Week, an annual tradition for the 82nd.

After a long wait Kate saw a doctor who examined her and concluded that she likely had a virus. He told us to take her home and return if her fever didn't ease the next day. A few hours after we got home, in the middle of the night, Kate went into shock. I drove frantically back to the hospital while Melissa gave Kate CPR.

There's a special room in every hospital where people wait for doctors to come and tell them the news that someone they love has just died. It's an awful place. You enter as one person, filled with naïve hope, prayers, and fear, and you exit as someone else, someone with nothing, only the sickening awareness that you're alive and wondering what to do with yourself because someone you've never met before just told you the focus of your life is gone.

I called the battalion headquarters and let them know I would be absent from the parade formation that would take place in four hours. After that, Melissa and I went to the bathroom, and then we walked out of the emergency room and toward our car; its headlights were still on, and its doors were still open. We went home and slept for a little while.

In the morning some of my fellow officers came by the house. It was cluttered with Kate's toys and clothes. A soiled diaper was sitting next to her crib in her room. The officers' wives brought food, but we didn't eat. Nobody stayed more than a few minutes. That day and for a long time after Kate died, I didn't want to talk to anybody. I didn't think anyone could understand—or that I could explain—the anger and anguish I felt.

. . . .

Several years after Kate died I went to the funeral of John Lewis, a West Point classmate of mine. I knew him reasonably well at school. We had been opponents in boxing class and had lived in the same building for four years. We'd been through Ranger school together, and we had friends in common. The funeral was in a rural part of Virginia, just a few hours from my home, so when I learned of his death I drove down for the ceremony.

The funeral was held in an old country church on sharecroppers' land that had some connection to John's or his wife's family. I was one of only two white people in the church. When I arrived, just a few minutes before the start of the ceremony, the only remaining empty seat was near the front, next to John's sister.

The ceremony was nothing like the cold, ritualistic Catholic funerals I've been to before and since. This service was clearly a celebration of John's life. Every member of his family stood up before the congregation and spoke about him. Then at least forty more people—friends from home and classmates from West Point—stood up one by one and spoke. They talked about how they had met John and what his friendship had meant to them. They all mentioned his smile.

When the choir sang, everyone in the church joined in. Then one of John's closest friends played some music videos on a big-screen TV—country and western (really melancholy songs), John's favorite. Maybe it was the setting or the music or the sincere, kind words by so many people, but I was overcome with emotion. As John's sister handed me tissues and patted my shoulder to comfort me, I cried more than anyone in the church.

# GRADUATION DAY

STEPHEN KARL KLOTZ

AS A DAD, I was above average. Unlike lots of other guys, I stayed around. I cared, got involved, and gave it my best. So what did it get me? A silent house, tears on my pillow, and a heart that felt hollow for a long time.

What happened? My children grew up.

Present and involved I was for my two boys. I assisted in their births, changed and cleaned *cloth* diapers, and read books—often the same ones over and over and over. As they grew older, I happily built forts, threw snowballs and baseballs, volunteered at school, wrestled on the floor, and attended innumerable activities and events. I hoped that it would never end. For my sake, they could have stayed at ages nine and twelve for about twenty more years. Instead, they grew up.

My de facto retirement from active parenting occurred on June 4, 2001. Both sons graduated that day, the older one from college in the morning, the younger one from high school in the evening.

My older son moved to an apartment two hours away and began a teaching career. My younger one moved to a college dormitory, where he immersed himself in intense friendships and intellectual pursuits. Within a week of each other, they both moved out and on with their lives.

Meanwhile, I was back at the ranch house, with its empty rooms. On the first morning after my younger son left, his clock radio blared early, seeking to awaken him as it had so many times. I turned it off and then realized that it would stay silent for a very long time, perhaps forever. His bed was now the guest bed. My older son's room lost its bed, bookshelves, and desk. Twin recliners and a reading lamp replaced them. Familiar pictures and posters were gone from both rooms. Their walls awaited new, more mature decoration.

In our backyard, grass and weeds overgrew the lines of a volleyball court. The front door quit squeaking open and closed late at night, a sound that used to precede a young male voice tentatively saying, "I'm home." Juice and milk jugs in the fridge emptied at a much slower pace.

As a parent, you think that you'll have your kids forever. But at best, you share a few childhood years, and then they awkwardly shed that skin in adolescence and morph into new individuals labeled as adults. Both of my sons went on to move several times, get married, and establish themselves in jobs beyond the local area.

I can't say that I was surprised they left. My goal from the start was to guide my children toward being principled, capable, and confident adults. But I didn't know how hard releasing them to independence would be. After their graduation day, other factors—terrorist attacks and war, my divorce from their mother, surgery on my heart, and the death of my own father—made the letting go even more difficult.

Friends and acquaintances had lost children through death by illness and accident. Others mourned as drugs, alcohol, and other demons of self-destruction possessed their kids. This experience of mine wasn't as severe as any of theirs—not even close. Nevertheless, it left me sad, hurt, and lonely.

I looked for other guys who had been involved parents and now grieved because their children had left home, but I discovered a dearth of kindred spirits. I wondered aloud to friends, "Aren't there other dads who didn't desert, hurt, or take their children for granted while caring for them? Aren't there some older men who did more than contribute DNA, who deeply felt the impact of their children growing up? Aren't there any other fathers who have felt this loss like I have?"

The few people who reacted to my paternal pleadings gave perky pep talks and clichéd advice. Though well intentioned, they were not helpful. Rather, they invalidated my feelings and dismissed my distress. No one seemed to get what I was going through or know how to help me, except for one friend. After listening to me repeatedly complain about my plight, she said simply, "They're still your children, you know. They always will be."

They *were* my children, and I could be thankful they were alive and pursuing positive adventures. They weren't gone forever, nor had they run away from me. They had just walked away briskly, looking back and waving occasionally, while eagerly yielding to the irresistible pull of a wider world. I had helped to prepare them to do just that.

Part of me indeed was proud and grateful to present them to a world that badly needed their skills, energy, and passion for change. I could accept my retirement from one phase of parenting and feel good about it. I could now look forward to a phase in which my relationships with my sons would take on a different, deeper dimension.

We have grown closer. In recent years, our phone calls, e-mails, and visits have assured me that I have an important place in their lives, that I have not been forgotten as a father. We've shared news, advice, and plans. We've celebrated accomplishments and dealt with difficulties together. We've even confronted and confounded each other at times, but we have always returned to an abiding mutual trust, respect, and love. And sometimes, we still play catch in the summer and throw snowballs in the winter.

---

# BIRTH OF A FATHER

JOEL SCHWARTZBERG

TWO OR THREE NIGHTS A WEEK for the first few months of my son's life, I would click him into the backseat of our minivan and drive him to sleep. Lulled by the steady hum of tires on pavement, Charlie would conk out within ten minutes, but I would continue driving until I reached the nearest Dunkin' Donuts with a twenty-four-hour drive-through window, nearly an hour away.

A chocolate doughnut I could chomp while driving, but the jelly one required two hands, so I'd pull into a parking spot to eat. But stopping the minivan often roused Charlie. "Don't wake up, man," I'd plead, looking into the rearview mirror as my son rubbed his eyes and stirred. "Give me one more bite, just one more."

These excursions allowed my wife some precious sleep, but as I volunteered for chauffeur duty more and more often—and came home progressively later each time—she and I both knew there was more to my trips than coping with her exhaustion or my thing for sweet snacks. Eating doughnuts was one of the few tiny, personal pleasures I clung to after my son was born. When Charlie was added to my life, it was as if I gave up nearly everything in return, and the transaction left me reeling, like someone who had gambled away his soul.

I fell into a deep depression. But I didn't see it as an ailment; I simply saw myself as a weak, pathetic parent. When I saw other new dads and moms joyously spending time with their kids, I nodded congenially and swapped stories, but I felt terribly flawed and alone.

This was not what I expected from fatherhood, not after years of watching superdads strut their paternal stuff in sitcoms and seeing celebrity fathers declare their elation on *The Tonight Show* time and time again: "Jay, the day my son was born was the happiest day of my life!"

When my wife became pregnant, I expected to slide into fatherhood easily. "What's a little sleep deprivation?" I told myself. I got through college, after all. On the way to the hospital, I took the fantasy express lane, imagining we would leave the delivery ward with a clean, bubbly one-year-old—as the characters on soap operas sometimes do—instead of a wrinkly, oozy life-sucker.

In the hospital, fatherhood is easy, even if you're exhausted, because all the responsibility belongs to the nurses. Want to see the baby? Instant bedside delivery. Want the kid gone? No problem; just hit the call button. When you're not being visited by the obstetrician, the pediatrician, your family, or your rabbi, the maternity staff does it all. But they don't come home with you.

Within forty-eight hours after we returned to our apartment, the truth dawned on me: My life as I knew it was gone. Movies? Gone. Full nights of sleep? Gone. Indulgent showers? Gone. Sex was locked away in a time capsule and buried deep. The baby invaded every aspect of our lives, even taking up residence in our bed. My wife and I became slaves to this tiny new thing living in our home, and there was no going back. Ever.

A couple of days after my wife and I brought Charlie home, I conference-called my colleagues at the public relations firm where I worked. "How are you doing?" they asked excitedly, envisioning their own homes someday populated with clean, bubbly one-year-olds.

"It's good, well, OK," I said. "I'm very tired. Actually, it's very, very hard. I'm not sleeping . . ." I was close to tears, and the call ended quickly. My colleagues told me later that I had scared the crap out of them. I'm sure at least a few of them went back on contraception.

After a few days, once the initial shock of parenthood faded, my body got used to the sleep deprivation, and a new normality set in. I at least was able to look at my son and wonder, "This guy doesn't walk, speaks only nonsense, and can't even use my credit cards; could he really be ruining my life?" I was trying to counsel myself into becoming responsible, waiting—hoping—for paternal instincts to kick in. "Fake it till you make it," therapists say. But faking it was exhausting.

At some point toward the end of that eternally long week that I took off from work following Charlie's birth, I sat on the hardwood floor next to my son, both of us exhausted and craving a more comprehensible reality. Charlie started crying, and then I joined him. We didn't just cry; we bawled. Charlie, I assume, was lamenting the endless cycle of tease and confusion that was his world. I was mourning the loss of my former life. As emotionally messy as it was, that shared sob was our first bonding.

I have an old photo from when Charlie was a newborn that shows both of us asleep on a sunlit bed. Our arms are stretched over our heads as if we're doing a stadium wave. I see the picture as incontrovertible evidence that Charlie wasn't a foreign interloper maliciously playing Hacky Sack with my life. He was a part of me, a time-sucking, sleep-stealing, delicious—not malicious—part of me. And what's more, he needed me. I just had to step outside myself, out of my hole, to see it.

# PLUM ISLAND

NORM APPEL

I DIDN'T WANT CHILDREN when Wendy and I married. I was afraid I wouldn't be a good father, and for good reason: Though I kept it secret, I was drinking a lot at the time and taking lots of pharmaceuticals—mixing everything. How could I have another child in the family when I was still a child myself? It wasn't that I didn't love children; it's just that I was terrified I would do something wrong if we had one. So it was five and a half years into our marriage before David was born. Twenty-two months later we had another boy, Michael.

David was a charming kid—handsome and bright—and he could get anyone to do just about anything. But there was something different about him. During those moments when I held David, it was as if he wasn't really with me, as if his mind was somewhere else. A doctor once diagnosed him with dyslexia and hyperactivity disorder and pre-scribed Ritalin. We ended that relationship right away; we didn't want David on drugs.

. . . .

My honest working career lasted from 1959 until 1976. I was an early investor in the cable TV industry, among other ventures. In 1977, Wendy and I divorced, and I retired from the business world completely. I was forty at the time; David was eight and Michael was six. I had joint custody of my sons—one week on and one week off. The first week that I had the kids, I took them to Disney World. The following week, when Wendy had custody, I danced at Studio 54 for two days straight, except for a two-hour break.

I eventually got into acting and modeling and would spend a lot of time hanging out at the old Travis Restaurant on Newbury Street in Boston, holding court and taking calls on the pay phone from my agent. I lived at the Copley Plaza hotel and then moved into a two-bedroom apartment at the Prudential Tower.

When they were with me, David and Michael stayed in the bed-room next to mine. The boys knew I was an alcoholic and a drug addict, so whenever I left my apartment, I would dead-bolt my bedroom door and lock my bedroom closet to keep them from finding my pills. But by the time he was ten, David knew where I kept the drugs and how to get to them. In his bedroom, he removed the heating grille and found a way through the ductwork into my room. Once in my bedroom, he would pick the lock on the closet. I figured this out after a friend of mine, who was staying at the apartment, saw David in the ductwork. She saw him as she was stepping out of the shower.

David began living on his own when he was sixteen, in an apart-ment in Boston not far from mine. Soon after moving into that apart-ment, he overdosed on drugs. We took him to the hospital, where they pumped his stomach. At about this same time I finally had enough of my own drinking and drugging and stopped. But I couldn't do anything to help David.

Twenty years later, I've become friendly with the woman who

lived in the apartment across the hall from David's during those years. She has told me how her mother wanted to adopt him. She remembers David as the sweetest, most lovable kid. But she also told me how he would break into my apartment, get my keys, and take my car to pick up Michael at school. She, too, knew he was wild.

. . . .

David had a wonderful artistic sensibility. He pursued photography and went to Hawaii to work on his craft. He returned to Boston two years later, landing at my apartment and talking about a show he hoped to have presented in Provincetown through a connection he had made with Diane Arbus's daughter. I never knew if he was telling the truth about the show, but within forty-eight hours he was driving me crazy, bringing people home at all hours of the night to that bedroom where he had climbed through the ductwork. Wendy had bought a tiny, two-bedroom shack on Plum Island, about an hour away on the North Shore of Massachusetts, so I told David to go there and stay for a while.

A couple of days later, I was shopping at the mall next to my apartment when I bumped into Wendy. She was on her way to lunch with a friend. We said hello to each other and went our separate ways. Then my cell phone rang, and it was Michael, my younger son. He had gone up to Plum Island to see David and found him in bed, not moving.

I found Wendy at the restaurant, and we drove to the shack. When we arrived, police cars were parked outside. We would learn that David had died of an overdose of prescription drugs. He didn't leave a note. I went into the shack and opened the door to the bedroom where David was. But I couldn't look at him. I couldn't bear seeing him dead. So I closed my eyes and shut the door.

. . . .

David used to tell me that Michael was the one with the drug problem, but I didn't think there was a chance of that. Then I came home one afternoon not long after David had died and found Michael on the walkway in front of my apartment building. He was hanging over the railing, unconscious. I tried to wake him. I tried to get him to walk. He looked horrific. I took him to the hospital, and the doctors told me he was in bad shape, that he'd been doing a lot of heroin for a long time.

Two days later, in the middle of the night, Michael left the hospital, walked out the front door in his johnny, and headed down the street toward his mom's apartment, which was nearby. She wasn't home, and the doorman wouldn't let him in. So he walked back to the hospital, broke into a medicine cabinet, found something he liked, and shot it into his arm.

When I reached the hospital, a doctor was placing defibrillator paddles on Michael's chest. I watched as the doctor jolted him with electricity, but Michael didn't respond. "How the fuck is this happening to me?" I said to no one in particular. This was why I didn't want to have kids.

The doctor put the paddles on him a second time, and Michael's heart began beating. The doctor told me he didn't know if Michael would make it through the night. He said I could stay if I wanted to, but that if Michael did live, he wouldn't know where he was for days. I went home, and when I returned in the morning I found out Michael was still alive.

· · · ·

Michael amazes me. Over the last decade he has rebuilt his life around helping other people, devoting himself to saving drug addicts through interventions. Wendy seldom returned to the shack on Plum Island after David's death, but Michael and I visited it regularly. Both of us wanted to keep the property in the family, so Wendy gifted it to Michael. I helped him design a new house that has since replaced the shack. It's on the beach—three bedrooms and as much floor space as my apartment. It's simple but gorgeous.

Years ago, when David was on his way back from Hawaii, he had stopped in Los Angeles for a day and met some friends. He was having lunch at an outdoor café in Beverly Hills when a stranger came over to his table and asked David if he could draw him. David apparently said yes and gave the artist Wendy's home address. David died two weeks later, and then two weeks after that an envelope arrived in Wendy's mailbox. It was a lovely black-and-white line drawing of David, signed and sent from California by an artist who turned out to be one of the head animators at Walt Disney Studios. Michael and I had that image tattooed on our backs, and we hung the original drawing at the entrance to the house on Plum Island. We spread some of David's ashes on the beach in front of the house and keep the rest in an urn by the fireplace.

I spent last Thanksgiving and Christmas on Plum Island. Michael visited the night before Thanksgiving. It was just the two of us. We ate dinner, and then we sat on the little second-floor balcony, smoking cigars, looking out over the beach, and watching the ocean.

# THE ACT YOU'VE KNOWN FOR ALL THESE YEARS

### STUART HORWITZ

WE WAKE UP DAY AFTER DAY to the sound of our daughter singing somewhere in the house. On different mornings, we take her singing to mean different things. We tease Fifer about how perfect everything is, and she'll say, "I admit it. I love my life!" Underneath this repartee is a sadness that Bonnie and I try to keep from becoming real jealousy. We envy her unconscious joy in living, the ability a ten-year-old has to just brush off the hurt and wake up singing. Other days, her singing reminds us that she is a unique individual, a product of her parents, but with something else mysterious thrown in.

It used to drive me insane that my daughter didn't like to read. She could; she would. She just preferred to cut designer fashions out of paper and adorn them with tiny beads and messy glue. Me, my whole life is words. I coach writers, I teach writing, I write. From an early age I saw myself as an incarnation of genius whose work would someday be housed between Hesse and Huxley on the library bookshelf. When, in my adolescence, I confided my literary dreams to my dad, he did his best to undermine them. "If you go to law school," he said, "I'll pay for it, but if you get a graduate degree in English, you're on your own."

He knew what he knew; I know what I know; he was not particularly predetermined to set his offspring free, and neither am I.

Then something happened in my mid-thirties, when my daughter was six or seven: I stopped reading. I brought crates of novels to a used-book store and traded them for a T-shirt. I started to look at the world more directly, without the filter of black lines across white pages. I picked up the guitar. How sweet it was to make music, to bang on strings and sing to myself—this simple lesson I learned from my daughter on those mornings when I had ears to hear. No one was recording me; I wasn't going to make a name for myself. Something even better was emerging: I was alive.

· · · ·

One day, when Fifer was eight, we received a notice that our local community center was hosting tryouts for *The Wizard of Oz*. For the auditions, kids had to sing a song without any accompaniment. My daughter learned "Somewhere Over the Rainbow," with help from her grandmother and Bonnie, and then they trundled off to the audition.

"They wouldn't even let me be a Munchkin," Fifer said upon her return, with a disappointment that was not tinged with bitterness, if an adult can imagine such a thing. And this is a kid with perfect pitch. I'm not bragging, because her talent doesn't come from me. We had started learning some songs together, with me on the guitar and her on vocals; I would look over at the tuner, during an obscure part of the Beatles' "Within You Without You," for instance, and she would be right there on the B-flat. I remember a friend of hers, a kid symbolically named Dylan, once asking her, "Why are you always singing?" Fifer replied, "Because it's my destiny."

Besides being fated to become a vocalist, my daughter loves money (she's a Capricorn). To see this trait so apparent in a child's eyes was a little shocking, but it gave me an idea: We would step it up on the songs we had been practicing—which made me happy, fulfilling my role as the father who was supposed to make her stick with things—and then we would play them on the streets for money. Busking is what it's called; we learned that term together. "Some dads take their kids fishing," Bonnie said. We would perform *Sgt. Pepper's Lonely Hearts Club Band* straight through twice (with the exception of tracks two and four, which we never got around to learning). Though Fifer vowed me to secrecy—she wanted to keep her "normal girl" status, playing softball (pretty well) and viola (no worse than anyone else in third grade)—she looked forward to our "gigs" as much as I did.

Her enthusiasm for performing didn't surprise me. One time when she was about three, we attended a crowded story time at the local library. After the reader had stepped down, Fife crawled between all the sprawled-out kids and patient parents and got into the big chair. Then she picked up a book. "Now it's my turn," she said. She couldn't read yet, so she sort of performed the book by looking at the pictures. The reader, an older gentleman who was vaguely famous, came over and clapped me on the shoulder. "I've never seen that before. Good luck, Jack."

Maybe it was genetic. In my early twenties, as a performance poet, I had stood in front of the American Express office in Prague after dawn, declaiming Bob Dylan lyrics, with a hat placed on the sidewalk to collect tips.

· · · ·

Busking is a genuine artistic experience. No gatekeepers determine whether you're good enough; the audience does. People either dropped money into our guitar case or they didn't. Some, like the crowd outside Fenway Park, were surly and drunk and not into having their hearts moved by a young girl. Others were encouraging, like the woman who told Fifer, "Jesus loves you, honey." Fife turned to me, and without a trace of irony, said, "That's so nice!"

We had hecklers. My ex–business partner said, "You're teaching your kid to beg, huh?" But in what other job can an eight-year-old make over $300 in one summer? Fifer gave some of the money she made to charity, and she put some in the bank for a car, but then she bought herself a powder blue iPod Nano, for which I paid only the tax. It was a proud moment in my parenting career.

We didn't do it for the money, of course. There were times when we would be walking to our spot, and one of us would freak out a little and ask, "Why are we doing this again?" And the other one would respond with what became our mantra: "To face our fears!" We did it for that moment after we had set up our music stands, when we had taken a deep breath and were looking around for a sign that we knew wasn't going to come from anywhere but inside us. And then we would start.

I can hear Fife now, imitating Paul: "One! Two! Three! Fo! [We're Sergeant Pepper's Lonely Hearts Club Band / We hope you have enjoyed the show . . . ]" It was always easier when a few people she knew were in the audience; then if, for instance, the high-E string on my electric guitar broke during "Lovely Rita," we could get other people to sing and clap along. Other times Fife couldn't get started at all. That's when I would forget about the weight of the amps that I had to carry and forget about my own need to be heard, which was always lurking. I would be ready to pack it all up again if I had to, and I'd offer to do so. Then maybe the cloud would pass, and I could coax Fife back into connecting with her confidence.

"It always feels better to play than not to play," was one of the quotes Fifer wrote down from those days—she chronicled every show we did over the span of two summers. Besides the good lines, she recorded the set list, the screw-ups, the amount of money we made (of course), and the magical moments. She wrote about the time on Boston Common when we drew a crowd only after a dying pigeon named Sam did his diseased circle dance in our guitar case. Then there was the time we had just finished a set of *Sergeant Pepper's* and an eleven-year-old girl came up to Fifer and asked, "Did you write those songs?"

Some things she didn't write down. My father and mother came to see us and listened as we performed "She's Leaving Home." I sang John's chorus: "We struggled hard all our lives to get by . . . What did we do that was wrong?" I'm not sure how much of the healing my father and I were doing was conscious, but afterward he bought me a state-of-the-art portable recorder to capture our best tunes.

"What does that mean," Fifer asked, " 'She's leaving home after living alone for so many years'?"

"You will never know," I said.

The shows went on, and we had our ups and downs. There were great moments. A female drummer—Rachel—joined us, and she did the best-ever "Ah-ah-ah-aahs," in "A Day in the Life." A rhythm section—Robbie and Timmy—filled in for Rachel one night and then never left. My daughter, now nine years old, was fronting a Beatles cover band. Yeah, that made me proud.

Then there were nights when she wanted to go to church or a school party. But we had already made all of our arrangements, and you can't just cancel on other people at the last minute . . .

New York was probably our finest hour, blasting through a punk version of "Somewhere Over the Rainbow" in defiance to what had started the whole experience, or holding an a cappella sing-along during Bob Marley's "Redemption Song" (we had increased our repertoire by then). A guy named Adam approached us in Washington Square Park, offered us fruit, and called us "his lovelies." "You have helped me feel free again," he pronounced. Somebody else said they wanted to make a documentary about us.

And then Fifer said she was done. She gave no reason, until I pushed, and then her reasons kept changing. "There're too many kids here," she said one night in Newport, when we drove away from the town without ever playing a note. (Was she getting self-conscious now that she was approaching preadolescence?) Or she would say, "I'm bored." But how can you say that? You had your arms up in exultation after your last performance, squealing, "That was so fun!"

Then I recovered a little Zen. It is what it is. Stop asking questions. Don't accuse her of being lazy, not committed. Let it go and be there for her in the way she needs you to be. Keep learning the lessons at hand.

• • • •

Three months after our last gig, someone e-mailed us about an upcoming audition. The national tour of *Chitty Chitty Bang Bang* was coming to a stage much bigger than the one where *The Wizard of Oz* had played. Did she want to go try out? Because it was totally up to her; I wasn't going to take the rap as some pushy stage father. Yes, she said. And yes again, when I asked again later.

The ornate lobby was crammed with kids warming up for their well-taught dance routines. Eighty-six kids were trying out for seven spots. When a ten-year-old next to me belted out "Everything's Coming Up Roses," I thought it was Ethel Merman herself. "Well, it's a good experience," I told Fife. "Think about all the people who aren't even here. There's no way they're going to make it—right?—if they're not even here?"

Fifer was going to perform her last, best busking song, the one we would play over and over again in Central Park, when the tourists couldn't give two shits about us: " . . . And you, take me the way I am." They took the kids away in groups of ten, leaving us parents in the lobby.

"Tell me again how she said it?" I asked. Fife had returned to the lobby, and I wanted her to describe precisely how the judge had responded to her performance. Fife went through a few different intonations until she was satisfied with her delivery: "Wowwww!"

I was the first in the house to find out Fife had been picked for the part. I bought the *Chitty Chitty Bang Bang* DVD and played the theme song loud enough one November morning to wake everyone with the news.

That night, I wanted to watch the movie. "Dad," Fifer said, "the performances aren't until March."

Apparently I was still learning, about nonattachment, about doing the thing that is to be done in that moment, about being there for somebody even when what they need is changing too fast for conscious record. Then I settled into our rematch of Sorry! Sliders, trying my best to beat her, because that's how we do things around here.

# A DEATH AND A BIRTH

ROLF GATES

I WAS STAYING with my sister Wendy and her new husband one night when they got into a terrible argument. "I don't know what to do," I heard Wendy say. "I don't know what to do." Wendy's life had caught up to her.

The next morning her husband woke me. He was frantic. He dragged me to their room, where I found Wendy, dead. She was thirty-one years old. She had committed suicide, with the same determination and decisiveness that she had done everything else in her life. Moments later I was on the steps of their porch, listening to the sirens of the ambulance that was arriving too late. In rapid succession I was being questioned by police, then bringing the news to our parents, and then getting ready to go to a funeral.

My parents adopted Wendy from an orphanage in Korea in 1959, when she was six months old. She came to the United States extremely ill with tuberculosis and complications from that ailment. My parents loved her immediately and nursed her back to health. My older brother came some time later, also from Korea, and I was adopted in 1966 after spending the first two years of my life in an orphanage in Albany, New York. My first memory is of the night I was adopted. My new family and I were in a hotel room, and I became tremendously ill from the chocolate the nuns at the orphanage had given me as a gift. I woke up several times in the middle of the night to throw up more violently than I ever have since. After one of these episodes I lay down in my bed and realized someone was sleeping next to me. It was Wendy.

As a young woman, Wendy was smart, very funny, and almost always kind. She did not have the physical courage of an athlete; she had the moral courage of a leader. It was her fate to be a small Asian girl in a small white world. She was required to move through childhood and adolescence as a subhuman. To her family she was everything; to the rest of the world she was nothing. She bore this burden with unimpeachable courage and integrity.

My love for Wendy was a blend of reverence, hero worship, and delight. She knew all of my failings and loved me fiercely nonetheless. I could screw up a thousand times and she would be there the next day expecting me to do my best. There was never a moment when I did not want to impress her.

At the funeral home, I stole a moment to be alone by Wendy's open casket. I did not know what I wanted from her. I touched her hand, refusing to accept what it meant that her hand was cold. I knelt to tell her how much I loved her, but anger overtook me, and instead I told her, "I will not die this way."

Wendy and I had lived in the addict's world, a world without hope of redemption. In that moment I left that world and began my sober life. I had been getting sober for six months. In that moment, I began living sober.

Living sober has meant remaining steadfast in the belief that our lives have a purpose, a destiny. It has meant being willing to continually learn and apply spiritual teachings to my daily interactions and circumstances. Living sober has meant never giving up.

Twelve years after Wendy's death I saw my daughter's head, then her face, and then her hands, and finally and miraculously her whole body emerge from her mother's womb and into the world.

Her name is Jasmine. She was born in May 2003. By then her daddy had become a success story. I was a yoga teacher and businessman and devoted all my time to both. I had emerged from my sister's death extremely focused. I was determined to stay sober and to use my remaining days in the service of the God of my understanding. Everything else was just a means to that end.

In the years before my daughter was born, people sometimes would say I had a big ego, that I was intimidating, that I did not listen, or that I was arrogant. But I did not care. I was teaching yoga to a hundred people a day, and each week the teachers I supervised taught three thousand. This was part of my mission, and the mission was all that mattered.

A few days after Jasmine was born, my wife asked if I could hold the baby while she took a shower. I was dumbfounded: Why should I be implicated if my wife decided to take a shower? If I had a motto at that time it would have been the advice a father of five once gave me: "If you want to get anything done, leave early and leave alone"—emphasis on *alone*. The next few months were very bad between my wife and me; everything was a problem. The next couple of years were pretty bad; most things were a problem.

Yoga teaches us that our lives are in constant transformation, the old ways dying to make way for new ones. The Buddha taught that our resistance, our clinging to the old ways of being, causes us to suffer. In the first months of my daughter's life, in the first months of my new life as a father, I clung to my old life.

I clung to the way I spent my time, to my freedom to choose how my day unfolded, to my alone time with my wife, walks with my dogs, nights of unbroken sleep. I clung to the person who I thought I was. The Buddha said that to resist what is, burns like fire. In the midst of my success story I burned like fire. My wife and I went to couples counseling and talked a lot about my failings, but I continued to cling to my ideas of how I thought things should be.

Jasmine was not fazed by any of this. She came into this world to have a great time, and she set about that goal with a passion. She was talking and walking at eleven months and spent her days exploring and learning. Each night before bed, she and her mom would look at pictures of all the people in her life and she would name them all. Then they would sing a lullaby that listed all of the people who loved her. In a card she made for Jasmine at the end of kindergarten, her teacher wrote, "I will never forget the joy and enthusiasm you bring to everything in your life."

When we expose darkness to the light it becomes light. I had a choice: the darkness of holding on to the old ways or the light of the family my wife and Jasmine were offering me. My old ideas continued to make sense to me, until a friend told me about a nine-day retreat he had just completed at a meditation center in Massachusetts. He spoke enthusiastically about the experience, and a couple of months later I went on my first meditation retreat. That was a few years ago, and since then I have been like a snake shedding its skin.

On my first couple of retreats I was aflutter, bouncing between self-recrimination and self-justification. But sitting quietly, doing nothing, I began to settle down. I developed the ability to concentrate, to soften, to be still, to listen, to feel, to be curious, to learn, to understand. I eventually made peace with myself, and once I could accept myself, everything else became workable. I could start where I was. I was an orphan who grew up in a family of orphans, who now needed to learn to be a part of a family.

On these retreats I would spend nine or ten days silently learning to have a relationship with myself. I would come home and discover that I could use those same skills to build my relationship with my family. My family is constantly growing and changing. It does not ask for my permission to do so; it just does, and then it looks over its shoulder to see if I am coming along. The skill I have learned in stillness and in silence is to be a friend to myself. Within the space of my own kindness I can let go of my clinging and try new ways of being.

The death of my sister was a shattering experience. When I collected my broken parts I recast myself in steel. The person who was born from that death was unyielding. In my grief it felt good to be implacable.

But Jasmine has taught me the value of suppleness. I have found that the ends may indeed justify the means, but our experience, what we live, is the means. My family is the means. My life is the means. The end is just death.

A teacher of mine says that the ordinary is the way. The shining path is the care that we bring to the everyday. I am learning to touch life as though it was something exquisite, something fragile, something beautiful. I am learning to remember Wendy and to remember Jasmine with each breath.

# BEING THERE

## CHRISTOPHER KOEHLER

THE DESIRE TO KILL MYSELF forced me to man up, deal with my depression, and be present in my own life and in my son's.

By the time I was thirty, I had overcome a major bout with depression. It emerged during my last year of graduate school. While my husband was at work, I would sit in our living room and sob. There wasn't a reason, and there seldom is with major depression; it's not a disease that lends itself to intellection. It brings an impenetrable morass of despair that changes how you think. I can't explain why I hurt; I can only hurt, and push away those who try to help.

I inherited the disorder from both sides of my family, generations of dour German Protestants who gritted their teeth and soldiered on. But I was determined to be the last one. I decided around that time that the family line would end with me, that mine was a genetic heritage not worth passing on—however unlikely it was that a gay man would sire a child.

In my early thirties, I arranged my life more or less the way I needed it to be. The things I had not yet actualized were in progress. I was at the center of a large group of nonbreeding friends. I was self-absorbed and happily so. Then the depression returned, and it came with a new diagnosis: double depression, which is major depressive disorder stacked atop dysthymia, a persistent, low-grade, high-functioning depression. Even when I'm not depressed, I'm not happy. I endured a longer, deeper spell than the last one, but just as they had previously, medication and talk therapy eventually pulled me through.

Meanwhile, my husband was watching the calendar. He was approaching forty and knew that having a baby after forty meant crowding sixty by the time the offspring graduated from high school. Years earlier we had batted about the idea of becoming parents, but I hadn't heard much about it for a while. Now he was determined to have a child—soon. I still didn't want to be a parent, regardless of whether the child carried my genes, and so we had the first major fights in our by-then decade-long relationship. They were long, drawn-out, tense battles, with the two of us talking too much or not at all. Maybe I wouldn't pass on my depression to a child, but still, I never wanted to have to say, "Daddy can't. He's too sad."

Nevertheless, I accompanied my husband to an informational seminar on adoption, in 2001, on a date that would turn out to be almost two years to the day before our son was born. That we were a same-sex couple was irrelevant. We were long-term, stable, and solvent. We were good candidates to adopt. The decision to have or not have children includes no compromises; few choices are more starkly binary. I loved my husband more than I feared parenting, so I capitulated.

We essentially lived on my husband's salary while I stayed home with the kid. With the money we saved on child care, we actually came out ahead financially. But within months of bringing our son home, I was sunk deep in an emotional swamp. I felt as though everything that ever mattered had been stripped from me because the needs of an infant must come first. It's a bind that many women find themselves in, but that few men do, and support for men is correspondingly scarce.

My first brush with suicide came when my son was just a few months old. I sat at the kitchen table one night after dinner, my mind so mired in a fog that I barely knew where I was. I rolled a bottle of fizzy water back and forth in my hands, watching the effervescence through the blue plastic. I took a sip and felt the tingle as the water ran down my throat. I thought about pouring out the water, just to see it flow across the tabletop and hear it rain onto the floor. I couldn't think of a reason not to, and as I tipped the bottle, I also couldn't think of a reason not to slit my wrists. I imagined the blue water in the bottle as red water in the bathtub, and the fizz as the sting of the blade as it bit into my wrists. These thoughts should've scared the piss out me, but they didn't.

I didn't slit my wrists. Instead I limped along and eventually got a job outside the house. But by the autumn of 2008, I was depressed more often than not. I usually would be on a ladder the morning after Thanksgiving, applying to the house a tasteful selection from my large collection of Christmas lights. But not that year. Less than a week before Christmas, I realized we didn't even have a tree.

On Christmas Day my husband had to work, leaving me alone with the kid. I was morose and angry. I could hardly stand my own company, let alone anyone else's, including my son's. I needed to be alone, made it starkly clear to him that I would be alone, and then retreated to my study to do some yoga, leaving my son ensconced in front of the television and the DVD of *How the Grinch Stole Christmas*.

I hid in my study, trying to use yoga's manipulations of my body to jolly my mind into a state that might allow me to survive the gathering later that day with my parents and the rest of my family. Less than halfway through a short practice I heard, "Daddy, Daddy, Daddydaddydaddy." He wasn't crying, so I tried to ignore him, but he continued with a child's persistence. I was angered, even enraged, by the interruption. I just needed to be alone, for twenty minutes. Full of wrath, I flew downstairs.

"What!" I screamed as I slammed open the bathroom door.

My son, for some reason naked, was hiding behind the door, and it hit him when I opened it.

"I love you, Daddy."

"You called me down here for that?" I said, mocking, bitter.

Manhood is determined not by organs or genetics, but by actions, and in that moment, when all my son wanted was a little bit of me, I proved that as a man I had failed, and I knew it. I went to my bathroom and fell to the floor, wishing I could die, wishing I were already dead.

I knew, with absolute certainty, that if I had a gun, I would have used it on myself. From those depths came one clear thing: I had to deal with this, and I had to do it for my son. This was more serious than installing garden-variety neuroses in my child. To kill myself would be to fuck up my son permanently. A parent's suicide sets the kid up for life.

But there was so much else to deal with. My son had been acting like a beast. Daily talks with day care providers and endless domestic disciplinary issues had ground me down. I even consulted his pediatrician about medication. Fair was fair: If I had take drugs, he was going to, too, damn it.

Then I asked myself, who's the man? The answer was humbling. I was, in theory, and I needed to act like it. I knew that some of his behavior was of my authorship. He was five, not yet old enough to have developed truly bad habits, not yet capable of the self-analysis needed to understand what he must have felt. Reacting and acting out were the only means of expression he had. I'd been the at-home parent for most of his life, and I was emotionally and physically absent. Part of the answer to his behavioral questions was me. I was his father, and the man, and it was time to be both. I no longer had the luxury of being melancholy.

I've always been a fan of the fake-it-till-you-make-it school, so I applied its principles to parenthood. I forced myself to be glad, even thrilled, whenever I was around my son. Every time I saw him, I hugged him. The little guy is surprisingly huggable, and I was one of the few he let hold him. First thing in the morning? Big hug. (He likes an audience when he gets up, like Louis XIV inflicting the levee on his court. So I made myself give His Little Majesty a minute or two before breakfast.) Picking him up from his grandparents' house after school? Big hug and a smile, even if I didn't feel like giving either. Before bed? More hugs, plus cuddling over stories. The kid showed his face, and there I was, trying to squeeze the stuffing out of him.

Then a funny thing happened. Faking it turned into the real deal. I'm still not sure when it happened, but I became glad to see him, genuinely glad. At the end of the day, I'm still tired, and he still talks too much. I'm still frustrated by the kindergarten dawdling, but it's not the martyring experience it was even a few months ago. Thus freed, I now participate more in my son's life. It's easier to give of myself, to read to him, to play with him, to listen, which is what he wants most of all.

That moment of fatherhood failure made me realize that I had to live even as I longed to die. It made me begin to heal, and in healing, to be there for my son as the father he deserves. Or at least to try.

# CRASH AND LEARN

TOM MATLACK

I WOKE TO THE SOUND of metal scraping against pavement. Sparks brightened that otherwise gray winter day in 1991. I was hanging upside down inside my girlfriend's baby blue Ford Escort, suspended by a seat belt as the car hurtled at sixty miles per hour along the westernmost section of the Massachusetts Turnpike.

I was twenty-six at the time. I had been in New York City with my girlfriend the night before, taking a break from my grad studies at Yale and drinking until dawn. While she took a train home to Albany, I had gone to class in New Haven, still drunk, and then set out for Albany myself. On the thirty-mile stretch of the Mass. Pike between Westfield and Lee you see nothing but pine trees and the occasional white-tailed deer. Somewhere along that span I drifted into a peaceful sleep.

I remained calm as the car slid along on its roof. There was nothing to do but wait and see what would happen next. The sensation was familiar. I had long been a human missile with no guidance system. One summer evening, just for fun, I'd lifted a love seat over my head and tossed it out an eighth-floor window of a UCLA dormitory; one New Year's Eve, just before midnight, I was thrown through the plate glass window of a midtown Manhattan restaurant, to the horror of the foursome whose dinner I landed on; I'd been accepted at the Tuck School of Business at Dartmouth and then was thrown out, before attending my first class, for lying on my application; and I had developed a habit of blacking out from drinking.

I felt a searing pain as the roof of the car, slamming against the turnpike an inch from my head, crimped around a clump of my hair and yanked it from my scalp. The seat belt dug into my chest, drawing blood that stained my shirt. At last, the car stopped, leaving a wake of scrapes in the pavement. I unbuckled, fell on my head, and screamed, "Fuck!" After forcing the door open with my shoulder, I sprinted away from the car, afraid the gas tank was going to blow.

We have a remarkable ability to respond instinctively to life-threatening danger. The problem comes after that initial, instinctive response: The body shuts down. A state policeman found me shaking violently on the side of the highway. I still can't remember what happened after I got out of the car. I could have been standing on the side of the highway for thirty seconds or for thirty minutes.

"Son, you're one lucky son of a bitch!" the trooper screamed while shaking his head in disgust. "I've seen plenty of Escorts flip, but I've *never* seen anyone survive. I don't like having to pull dead bodies out of wrecks, so how about being more careful?"

His words didn't register. I had beaten death again.

· · · ·

In my budding business career, as the stakes grew bigger, I brought the same sense of invincibility and calm that I had felt hurtling along upside down in the Escort. At twenty-nine, I became chief financial officer of the Providence Journal Company, a huge and fiercely private media conglomerate. The company's other executives, most of them twice my age, thought I should be getting them cups of coffee. I spoke only when spoken to. I sat attentively with my boss, the chairman of the board, as he drank Scotch and smoked cigars, rarely saying a word except to nod my head in agreement. And yet, once I had become his most trusted adviser, I needed just ninety days to take the oldest newspaper company in the country public and then negotiate the sale of the business in an Atlanta hotel room for billions to a bunch of cowboys from Dallas. The chairman had initiated the contact but never thought I could negotiate such a good price. When I did, he had no choice but to proceed, despite the firestorm it would cause among shareholders, employees, and the community. I stood to make several million dollars and be credited with pulling off the impossible.

My calculus at work had been flawless. After the sale, I appeared on the cover of the *Wall Street Journal*, a blond-haired wunderkind. What I had failed to calculate were the risks I was taking at home and how much I had to lose. I had two baby children, and I was about to learn how precarious my relationship with them really was. It was as if the car crash had put the emotional part of me into suspended animation. I was fearless in my professional life but unable to feel anything in my personal life.

· · · ·

Christmas that year was agonizing. My soon-to-be-ex wife had kicked me out of the house for good. My nine-month-old son, Seamus, and two-year-old daughter, Kerry, went to Albany with their mom. I was not invited. I packed a huge red fire engine in my company car, got on I-95, and drove to my parents' house in Washington, D.C. On Christmas morning I gave my brother's oldest son the fire truck and tried to soak up his enthusiasm. It didn't work. All I could think about was my own children waking up without me, on Seamus's first Christmas. My brother and sister and parents all were understanding and overly friendly, but I couldn't stop thinking about how I would never have the chance to live with my kids.

The next day, on my way back to Providence, I stopped in

Manhattan to smoke cigars with some college buddies. I had been trying to stop drinking without much success. That night my friends and I ended up in a SoHo restaurant with a mirrored bar that let all the beautiful people enjoy good views of themselves. It wasn't my worst night of drinking—I didn't flip any cars or fly through any plate glass windows—but I was rude and more than a little lecherous.

I woke up the following day with a pounding headache, the smell of cigarettes in my hair, and the taste of cigars on my tongue. I spent the morning contemplating how I could kill myself quickly and painlessly. But later in the day, as I drove back to Providence, I convinced myself that neither Seamus nor Kerry deserved the shitty father I had been. They certainly didn't deserve a dead father who didn't have the guts to face his demons.

That was the last time I had a drink, but sobering up was just the start. I had to learn how to take care of my two babies by myself. When their mother moved back to Boston, I knew I had to follow. But I had trouble finding a place that felt right to me, because moving out of my week-to-week hovel in Providence would mean that this was to be a permanent condition: I really wasn't going to live with my kids.

I eventually found a penthouse on the corner of Commonwealth and Massachusetts avenues, a killer bachelor pad to be sure, but not the dream I had in mind, so it took quite a while for me to settle in. The bathroom had a skylight over the tub, and often, when I couldn't sleep, I would take a bath and gaze up at the stars. The apartment faced east, toward the city core. From the seventh-floor bay window the views of Boston's brownstones and parks looked positively European. Each morning I meditated in the bay window until the sun hit the State House's gold dome in the distance and eventually made its way to warm my face. This perch became my monastery.

My ex-wife and I agreed that the kids would come to my apartment every Friday night. I put bunk beds and a matching wooden toy chest in what would become their room. Each week I'd pick up Seamus and Kerry, and all their gear, and drive around my city neighborhood looking for a parking spot. The kids were usually grumpy and hungry by the time I finally parked the car and loaded them into their double stroller. I'd put their bags on top and start pushing. I was driven by adrenaline, trying to make this all OK for them. By the time I had reached my building, unloaded the kids, and got them through the door and into the lobby, I would feel as though I had climbed Mount Everest. I'd tell Kerry to hold Seamus's hand, and then I would go back outside, collapse the stroller, and lug it up the stairs and into the lobby before corralling the kids into the elevator. From the elevator, the kids would run ahead down the hall. I'd catch them just in time to open the door to my apartment and lead them up a final flight of stairs inside. Then it was time for me to make dinner.

The first night I had the kids on my own I gave the them baths, slipped them into matching footie pajamas, tucked Kerry into her bunk, and then warmed a bottle for Seamus. In my bedroom, I turned off the lights and rocked him gently while he drank. I inhaled deeply. It was the scent of my son that changed everything—his scent and the sound of him suckling his bottle, the softness of his skin and the sensation of holding him as his body gradually went limp with sleep. I looked down and realized that this—being a father—was my deepest satisfaction. Chasing Kerry around the house at five the next morning, catching her, and tickling her as she screamed with joy confirmed it.

. . . .

In the days that followed my kids' first overnight visit, I realized just how much work I had to do as a dad. I feared I would never be a decent parent no matter how hard I tried. When they were at my apartment, my childhood fear of heights returned. I often had nightmares of the kids falling out the bay window. Kerry didn't help matters. Even at age three, she loved to taunt me by standing on the ledge inside that window with her nose pressed against the glass, looking out at the city and giggling at my discomfort. To set my mind at ease, I nailed two-by-fours across the bottom of the window.

I didn't want to see my kids just on weekends. During the week I took them to a playgroup in one of the buildings on Newbury Street. I sat in a circle with the moms and their kids, singing, wrestling, and generally acting goofy. As I rolled around on the floor, the moms didn't know what to make of me. But they gradually accepted me, and I got to be with my kids. On Saturdays I took them to the top of the Prudential building, only a few blocks from my apartment. The carpeted floors and large, soft furniture were ideal for some safe roughhousing, and the observation deck was a large square track, where the kids could wear themselves out by running around and around. There were rainy days when we couldn't see a damn thing, but we still went up there, just to have something to do together.

Care objects were very important to the kids as their little minds tried to manage all the moving around. Kerry had a blanket she slept with every night. Seamus became attached to a stuffed Pal dog from the PBS show *Arthur*. Pal took on identifying textures and wear marks as he was beaten, barfed on, and laundered. He was one of a kind and not replaceable. I became obsessed with knowing where Pal and "Blankie" were at all times. At the time, I kept a bag full of the kids' things in my room and doled out clothes and toys like gold bullion. As the end of each visit approached, I turned the apartment upside down with drill-sergeant precision to insure all the kids' stuff was accounted for.

Then one day Pal disappeared. I scoured under beds and behind furniture. The apartment wasn't that big, so coming up dry convinced me that the crisis was indeed serious. After several nights of listening to my tearful son on the phone bemoaning the loss of Pal, I slunk over to FAO Schwarz and purchased another.

I brought the replacement Pal to my office. I tried to duplicate, in a single day, years' worth of wear marks. I took a baseball bat to the pristine doggie, and then I threw the six-inch-thick *Handbook of Fixed Income Securities* at him. My partners in our venture firm couldn't figure out what was going on. My door was shut and I didn't respond to any calls or e-mails all day. On the walk home, I took the now-limp dog and rolled him in sidewalk sand. When I got to my condo, I threw him in the washing machine for an extra-heavy spin cycle.

That night I stood apprehensively at my ex-wife's front door with the new, but suitably worn, Pal. But before I could present him, I learned that the original Pal had been recovered: Kerry confessed to smuggling him home and hiding him inside the folds of her mother's curtains. When I returned to my apartment, I stored the spare dog in the back of my closet, just in case.

. . . .

Six years to the day after my last drink, I remarried. Elena and I had a son named Cole. I've been married now six years and sober twelve. Cole just turned four, Kerry is a freshman in high school, and Seamus just started junior high.

When Cole's eyes are heavy after a long day of pretending to be a knight, I get his jammie-joes on, brush his teeth, and he gives Mommy a good-night kiss and hug before I carry him in my arms down the hall to the cowboy-themed bedroom that Elena designed for him. We snuggle into the lower log-cabin bunk bed and read three books—about lost penguins, monkeys toying with alligators, and dogs wearing strange hats and driving cars.

Often Cole starts snoring before I have finished the first story. But sometimes he goes the distance. Either way, I turn the light out while still pinned between Cole and the wall. Even if he is already asleep, he stirs when he hears the switch and asks, "Daddy, will you stay with me for a little while?"

Holding my son as he slumbers on the bottom bunk, surrounded by big logs of raw pine, I feel cocooned and have to force myself to leave. I allow myself twenty minutes of forgetting what I was so anxious or mad or sad about before climbing in to read bedtime stories.

In the dark I listen to Cole snore as I stare up at the bottom of the top bunk, my mind empty of any thoughts. Every night some instinct eventually tells me it's time to get up and walk back into my life. But I return nourished just enough to make it through another twenty-four hours, until it's time to get our jammie-joes on again and climb back into the bunk beds.

SONS

# FIGHT OR FLIGHT

KENT GEORGE

SOMETIMES AS I WALK into my second-story office, I look out the window at a nearby tree branch and catch an unsuspecting squirrel in the middle of a meal. In that moment when the squirrel sees me, we both freeze for a long beat—he with his nut in his paws, me with my coffee in my hand. I look into his eyes and can see he's panicking: "Oh shit, oh shit, what now?" I identify with the squirrel's visceral reaction to the perceived threat: heart beating quickly, hair standing on end, adrenaline coursing through the veins—it's fight or flight.

The American physiologist Walter Cannon coined the term "fight or flight," sometime around 1920, to describe an animal's response to threats or acute stress. Though I have spent more than my fair share of time in a state of acute stress over one perceived threat or another, neither *fight* nor *flight* seem to capture my response. I have never been in a physical fight in my entire life. Truly. Though I'm not some sort of wimp; I have been in heated arguments, even shouting matches. But amazingly, I've never been in an actual physical fight.

I say *amazingly* because where I come from it wasn't easy to avoid getting into fights. I grew up in a very Irish Catholic family in a very Irish Catholic suburb of Boston, and let's just say that sometimes stereotypes exist because they're true. My people love to drink and fight. (I prefer to just drink.) To make matters worse, I grew up playing ice hockey, and hockey players like to fight.

But it wasn't my teammates who gave me the hardest time; it was my mother. See, my mother was a fighter. She loved to fight, and she loved and respected people who fought. She was like a hardened IRA terrorist who'd been dropped into a witness protection program in American suburbia. She'd drive around the town where I grew up, giving people the finger and then, if she got any reaction at all, jamming the brakes and looking in the rearview mirror at them: "Wanna go?" Oh yeah, and she'd get out of the car, too.

My mom was as tough as nails, but she was nothing compared to my sister, Lisa. My sister is one of those lesbians who was so ridiculously butch by about age seven that there was no denying her identity. They let her play Little League with the boys in my town in 1975, when she was nine, and even though she was the first girl ever to play, nobody said a word about it—at least not very loudly. I'm sure they were silenced by fear, but I'm not sure who they were more afraid of, my sister or my mother. Lisa was a fighter, too. She'd beat me and my brother both to within an inch of our lives. Of course there wasn't much of a challenge for my sister in fighting me, since I didn't fight back. I think she fought me mostly for the exercise.

I don't know what caused my pacifism. I'd like to say I had an early understanding of Ahimsa, the avoidance of violence, but that would be a lie. My pacifism wasn't political; it wasn't like I wanted to be Gandhi. I just didn't fight back. But I didn't run, either. That's the odd part.

• • • •

How would Dr. Cannon describe my reaction to acute stress in this situation? We're in the backyard. It's the middle of winter, early 1970s. I'm about five years old, and my sister is six, and she is throttling me repeatedly: blam, blam, blam! Mostly punches to the head. The kitchen window slides open, and my mother leans out with a cigarette in the corner of her mouth. I can tell she's furious. Mom watches silently for a bit, but my sister doesn't let up. She's throwing haymakers, jabs. She's alternating hands now because she's been hitting me for a good couple of minutes straight and she's getting a little tired.

When my mother finally speaks, it's to me: "For Christ's sake, chief, hit her! What the hell's the matter with you?" I had actually thought she was going to *stop* the fight. Believe me, any referee in his or her right mind would stop this fight: I've got my hands down by my sides, and I'm not trying to block or even avoid punches. My mom's got her fists balled up, and she's trying to show me what to do from the kitchen window. After a minute or two she just grunts, shakes her head, and shuts the window in disgust. Not fighting is one thing, but just standing there taking a beating is another.

It wasn't fight or flight, so what was I doing exactly? With my sister, my strategy was something akin to the rope-a-dope that Ali used on Foreman, except that I didn't make any effort to avoid the punches. I recall thinking, in a detached way, "It's not so bad. It hurts less than you might think it would. Plus, it'll be over soon. She'll get tired. Or bored. She'll stop eventually." And she did. See, what Lisa wanted was a fight, not just a workout. By not fighting back I took a lot of the fun out of it for her. As usual, she eventually moved on to my little brother. Though much smaller than me, he was the kind of kid who, when you hit him with a pitchfork or something, would fight back.

But while my sister would move on, my mom wouldn't give up on me quite so easily. She would try to goad and shame me into fighting. She'd go to my hockey games and scream at me at the top of her lungs. I guess people thought it was funny. I was a pretty good hockey player, mainly because I was fast enough to get out ahead on a breakaway or go into the corner and take the puck out and score a wraparound goal without touching anyone. And that made my mom nuts. As the rest of the crowd cheered after one particular goal, I could hear my mother above them all: "Oh, for God's sake, would it kill you to hit somebody! What is this, the fucking Ice Capades? I thought it was a hockey game!"

Following that game, in the car on the way home, she asked, "Are you gay? Seriously, are you gay? 'Cuz I have watched you play hockey for ten years now, and I don't think you've ever hit *anybody*. If you're a fag, it's okay. I'll get you some figure skates and one of those nice little dancing outfits. But if you're just a pussy . . ." She let her thought trail off, and then we drove the rest of the way home in a silence punctuated now and then by her epithets. I stared straight ahead blankly, taking it. She wasn't going to get my goat.

Despite our disagreements, my mom and I were tight, and we became drinking buddies when I was about fifteen. She'd take me over to the Ground Round or the Ninety Nine, and we'd hang out and drink and eat potato skins. Going to bars with my mother was a nightmare, though, because the minute we'd walk in, there'd invariably be some guy checking her out—some tough guy usually, some really drunk tough guy. And she'd look right at him and say, "What the fuck are you looking at?" I'd apologize and laugh sheepishly, and then, under my breath, I'd say, "Mom, leave it alone." But she'd ignore me and keep at the guy. "Yeah, you, tough guy, I'm talking to you! You got a problem?" Usually the guys knew her, and they would laugh, and often they'd even buy her drinks. But sometimes we'd run into a guy who took offense and wanted a fight—not with her, mind you, with *me*. It was a familiar feeling for me, being stuck in the middle of a fight.

· · · ·

I remember one time being in my bed—I'm about five years old now—and I hear a loud crash. There's a scuffle downstairs in the kitchen, and crazy, drunken arguing. (Why does it always happen in the kitchen, right under the bedroom where my brother and I sleep? Not that it would make much of a difference if it happened in another room, not in our tiny, two-bedroom house.) Then there is a *really* big noise. Is that the refrigerator going over? Man, no milk for my cereal tomorrow. Then silence. A long silence. I'm listening intently. Then I hear sobbing. Good, a sign of life. Then a door slams somewhere else in the house.

OK, they're both alive.

Then there are sirens; a neighbor has called the cops, I guess. The police and an ambulance arrive; even the fire department comes. I can't figure that last one out. There's no fire. But I don't move. Fire truck or no fire truck, I'm not going anywhere. There's lots more shouting. Mom's telling all the firemen to go fuck themselves. They take her to the hospital. Does somebody stay at the house with us? I can't tell. Maybe not, though that seems unsafe to me. I never move, though. Never. It's like with the riverboat in *Apocalypse Now*, when the captain says, "Never get out of the boat! Absolutely goddamn right!" You don't have to tell me, though. I'm not going anywhere.

Occasionally, before she runs away, my sister goes downstairs and gets right into it herself. "No, fuck you!" She jumps right up on my dad, tries to beat his ass. I hear a lot more scuffling for a while, and then for some reason it ends better than usual. Did the appearance of his eight-year-old daughter bring him to his senses? Or did she actually beat his ass? I'll never know. Through it all, my little brother just sleeps like a baby, in the bed next to me. How can he sleep through this?

When I'm older, I lie awake in my bed and listen to everything, and I can picture every detail. I hear Dad's car moving up to the house. Now he's in the driveway. I can tell he's drunk because he drops his keys twice on his way to the door. Then he opens the door. Wham! I can tell by the noise that Mom has been drinking at the kitchen table, and she has just launched the biggest piece of pottery she could find—some enormous, ugly bowl somebody gave her once, I suspect—straight at his head as he walked in. Would've killed a lot of guys, a big bowl like that, but Dad's got good instincts, and he gets a hand out in time to knock it down. Dad's also an ex-marine, and when he's attacked, he fights back.

They fight more and more often. It's a vicious circle. She's pissed off because he's gone so much, yet when he comes home she blasts him so hard that it makes him stay away longer the next time. That, plus the guilt and the shame, keeps him away even longer. Nobody else knows what he's dealing with. When she's walking around town with a black eye or a broken arm or a big cut on her wrist, it's obvious to everybody who did it; they know our family well enough to understand, though they don't know the whole story. Dad doesn't make any attempt to explain it to anybody, either.

. . . .

I didn't know the whole story myself—nobody did—until after my mom died at a fairly young age, and I learned that she had been severely mentally ill. Trust me, I always knew she was nuts, but when my sister was diagnosed with debilitating mental illness several years after my mother's death, I began to read about the illness and realized that my mother had suffered from, among other things, borderline personality disorder—a classic case of it. Borderline personality disorder apparently arises when infants don't develop "object constancy" at a certain stage. Object constancy lets you believe that things continue to exist even though you can't see them. So when my dad left the house every day, whether to go to work or just down to the corner store, my mom truly believed he had left her forever. And so when he came home, she went berserk on him.

Eventually, my dad did leave for good, of course. That's what tends to happen. Borderlines drive people away, though they would much prefer that you stay and fight. One of the biggest challenges we've had with my sister is that her doctors keep "firing" her. Most doctors will eventually stop seeing patients who are borderline, because borderlines are known to be so destructive to their own doctors' mental health. Nobody in his right mind would stick around. In our family, not only did my dad leave, but my brother and my sister both eventually ran away as well. When my sister was fifteen or so she went to live with her forty-year-old girlfriend in the city. (You can imagine how that went over with my very Catholic mother.) My brother ultimately ended up living at a friend's house.

So why didn't I leave? I could say it's tough to run away, that my brother and my sister were unusually tough kids. But the fact is I was paralyzed, checked out. Of course, it was tangled up with some weird Oedipal stuff, too; after her fights with Dad my mom often would end up in my bed with me. It was creepy. She'd have this blowout with him, and then she'd curl up in bed with me. Later she'd glower at me with her new black eye as if to say, "Think I might get a hand from you next time, Mr. Ice Capades?"

It turns out that animals respond to acute stress and perceived threats in many different ways, not only by fighting or flying. Some will stay perfectly still, so that predators will not see them. Other species have more exotic self-protection methods. In the end, it's all simply a matter of self-preservation. In my first-grade classroom we had a chameleon, and when it was explained to me how he adapted to survive, I was in awe. I identified with and admired him on a deep, instinctive level. I could imagine myself in a dangerous situation and thinking: "I'm just gonna change myself brown and stand over here by this tree and try not to breathe until it goes away." How nice it must be not to have to fight or fly, but also not to get caught. How nice it must be to have some neat little trick to escape with, like the opossum I found in front of my house one night, lying on the walkway. I went to get a trash bag to throw him away, and when I came back he was gone. That sneaky little fucker, he wasn't really dead.

Me, I just dissociated. I didn't have any trick. I couldn't blend into the trees like the chameleon or pretend to be convincingly dead like the opossum. So I just stood there in a state of suspended animation, like the deer in the headlights, like the crazy squirrel outside my office window, too startled to run, yet smart enough to know that fighting wouldn't make things any better either. If all else failed, I always had the old rope-a-dope. I could just lean into the ropes, take a few punches, and wait for my opponent to wear down, wait for the storm to pass. Sometimes that's the best you can do to survive.

# THE MOST IMPORTANT JOB

KEITH ACKERS

MIMI IS UPSTAIRS, gamely attempting to lull our three-year-old, Anna, to sleep, though it's still bright outside, and snowy. Anna abruptly stopped napping a couple of months ago, but we keep trying, realizing, as she can't, that she has been perpetually exhausted for weeks. It is tragic when a child inevitably discovers that if she tries hard enough, she doesn't really *have* to sleep. I fear she has inherited this rascal trait from her father.

I am safely downstairs, beneath the conflict, poking the fire, wondering how this lack of napping will affect us in the coming months. Mimi is seven months pregnant, and if memory serves, we're all about to be perpetually exhausted.

My eyes turn to the coals that have been glowing since I got home from a frigid trip to the park to try to wear Anna out a bit. This fire could be better.

I throw another log on, creating a brief volcanic explosion of sparks and smoke. The log isn't positioned right, so I reach right in to grab it, pulling my hand away just in time as a flame darts up to block my progress. I am taken back to my own father's fearless feats of fire making. I have remembered many of his spoken lessons: Always check the flue; small stuff on the bottom; leave lots of spaces for the air to get through your pile. I am routinely praised for my own fire-making skills and become disgusted with my effort if the thing does not burst into an immediate inferno upon lighting.

But I also appear to have adopted his belief that hands are made of iron, as I reach into the fire again and again with my bare hand, despite having arm's-reach access to an iron tool designed for this very purpose. Bah. My mother used to fret as Dad would do the same thing, warning him again and again not to burn himself. That was just a challenge, and I feel myself responding to it to this day, though my own wife seems not to share the concerns, accustomed as she is to my foolishness in general.

As a small boy, I was always drawn to the fire, in no small part because it meant I could see Dad at work, doing impressive things that I couldn't do. I would struggle to hoist a single log, but he could tuck six or seven under one arm and still keep the other hand free to work the door. He could not only make fire, he could reach right into it and never get burned. Incredible.

I was thrilled to be included in the process, asked to do what Dad said was The Most Important Job of wadding up the newspapers. This task was relatively calm as it applied to the starting of the fire, but it became fever pitched when the flames began to flicker and vanish and I was called upon to help resuscitate the dying patient. (Dad was *not* routinely praised as a great fire maker, but I now suspect that had more to do with lack of care of the wood, which was usually kept uncovered outdoors and was usually in some advanced state of decay.)

I have discovered in later life that building a successful fire is actually not that difficult and frankly not that impressive. More than once I've suspected that the women in my life have oohed and aahed over my abilities as they've watched from the couch, simply to stoke my ego and enjoy their tea.

But the inevitable smoldering and ensuing struggle didn't make Dad's fires any less impressive in my eyes. On the contrary, each fire became an epic battle. He would grab the corner of a smoky log between his index finger and thumb and throw it back onto the pile at a hypothetically better angle while barking, "We need more paper!" As I furiously crumpled, I would see him out of the corner of my eye, shaking his hand because sometimes those logs actually *were* too hot for mortal men to grab. And I would keep wadding paper as though the fate of that evening's comfort depended upon my speed and skill.

A small pile of newspaper balls would grow next to him as he crouched and blew into the ashes, ignoring the bellows that hung next to the hearth. The poker was strictly for jamming those little balls into the ashes, and he would not touch it a second longer than was necessary, dropping it with a clank as though it were hotter than the log he had just grabbed. Then, magically, one final puff would ignite the whole thing, and we could collapse and marvel at what we had done. Dad would usually be sweating, breathing hard, and wiping his sooty hands on his jeans. My own hands were darkened only by newsprint, but this was the apprentice badge of honor, so I didn't mind. Only then might Dad have time to reflect on the battle and occasionally show me the scar he'd just received, more than once explaining the bizarre smell that filled the living room as having come from a rogue flame that had singed the hairs right off his forearm.

When Anna is around now, I immediately appoint her to The Most Important Job, and she has taken the challenge, at three years old, with pride and gusto. In fact, if she catches me crumpling anything, she shrieks, "No, that's my thing!" and I must immediately relent. I marvel that I so naturally gave her this duty and she so naturally accepted it, and I struggle to remind myself to be patient on those occasions when her paper wadding is so careful and deliberate that I have to sit and wait for each agonizingly folded ball. But it reminds me that for all the failings I believe my father visited upon me, there were the occasional successes, inadvertent or not.

Fatherhood appears to be teaching me that, despite what I've believed for the past thirty-odd years, the quality of the fire doesn't matter. Nor is it important that you win the struggle and refuse to be beaten by any damn log, as my father seemed to believe. What matters is that you give your child the crackly warmth of knowing that his or her dad is impervious to amazing flames. And more important, you give her the belief that she is being brought along to one day be equally invincible.

Even though she really could use the rest, now I'm hoping Anna won't nap again today. This fire could be better.

# WHATEVER IT TAKES

RICARDO FEDERICO

"YOU LOVE THIS GIRL, RIGHT?" It was an unvarnished challenge, a test of no small order, and his eyes never left mine.

"Yes, I do," I said quickly. And I wasn't lying.

Never mind that I was twenty-four at the time and a U.S. Army veteran with an overseas tour of duty under my belt. There was still a tremor in my voice, because the man staring at me was—and always will be—my father.

Born in New York to Italian immigrants, he was a paratrooper in the 101st Airborne Division before going to work in construction. My mother died when I was young, and Dad raised my sister and me on his own. A broad-chested man with a flattop haircut, he could build, fix, or do anything he set his mind to, and he believed that jobs were to be done right. He had a penchant for introspection but also an Italian temper that could bloom quick and hot; he was not to be trifled with. These were not simply the observations of an impressionable boy; from a young age I paid attention to stories about Dad from his peers and family members. Small wonder, then, that admiration, respect, and a healthy dose of fear were my watchdogs throughout adolescence.

So it was that I went to see my father that winter in 1990, with his larger-than-life presence hovering over me still, to tell him I had met a girl, that I loved her, and that she was going to have my baby. My stomach was in knots, and I was sweating despite the cold, gray day. Dad had sold the house I grew up in while I was in the Army and bought a small travel trailer that he called home. We sat down at the little table, our faces not two feet apart, and I told him. I'm not sure exactly what I expected: disappointment, for one thing; judgment, perhaps; but severe admonishment for certain.

Dad looked across the table, his face a complex mask of concern for his son and the uncertain future, and his gaze pierced my young man's heart like only a father's can.

He held up a finger to stem any additional comment from me, and then he drew his breath to speak again. I braced myself, but what came next was not the browbeating I anticipated.

"Don't you leave this girl to do all the work," he began, with enormous, trembling gravity in his voice. "You take care of her, and you take care of the baby. You do whatever it takes, you hear me? You keep a job, you work hard, and you provide. Your buddies call and wanna go play basketball or drink beer, you tell 'em you got a family now. Sure, you go once in a while, but you be the first one back home, understand? Every time. You raise a family as a family, and these two—your girl and your baby—they're your responsibility now. You get what I'm telling you?"

"Yes, sir," I said.

He looked at me for a few seconds, the silence unwieldy after one of the longest speeches he had ever given me, and then he nodded. I think he saw what he was looking for in my eyes. He could tell that I got it, and that, even though I hadn't a clue what I was stepping into, I was earnest in my commitment. His face softened, and he put a hand on my shoulder.

"You'll be okay, then," he said. "You'll do fine."

And I believed him, as I always have.

. . . .

The next fall, my betrothed and I went down to the county children's services office to have our newborn daughter's last name changed to my own. I fumbled to unhook the car seat, a process still new to me, and shuffled through the fallen leaves with our child in tow.

So many things were changing so fast for us, and the future, while as mysterious and unfathomable as it always had been, was now tethered to something tangible and completely beyond our control: a new person who chose to eat, sleep, and do everything else on her own schedule.

When the clerk came into the office with the paperwork, she greeted my wife-to-be before casting a perfunctory glance my way. "Are you here on court order?" she asked.

I stood dumbly for a few seconds, not registering the meaning behind her question. "No," I finally muttered. "Why do you ask?"

"Oh," the clerk replied, a look of genuine surprise on her face. "I'm sorry. Most guys who come in to do what you're doing are here only because they've been ordered by the court."

*Guys*, she had said—not *men* and not *fathers*, just *guys*. It took a few minutes for the ramifications of that to sink in: guys who had to be forced by a judge to claim their children, if in name only. Then what? A lifetime of haphazard, court-ordered child-support payments while the mother works two jobs and scrapes by raising a fatherless child?

I sat, waiting to fill out the paperwork, and looked down at our new baby girl sleeping in her carrier. Seeing her like that, totally helpless and dependent, my face grew hot at the thought of being mistaken for one of those *guys*. In that moment I renewed my vow that I would not be anything less than a father to this child and a man for this woman I loved. I could do nothing less for them, or for my father, whose expectations for me were so clear and uncompromising.

We walked out of that office young, scared, determined— and together.

. . . .

My dad is retired now, and I've gotten to know him better over the years. And with that knowledge I've come to realize how narrow my perceptions of him had been. How many of us really know what our parents are about when we're kids? How can we, when we don't yet understand what they have done, what roads they have traveled?

Through lunches and long afternoon visits, I discovered many things about my dad. In his youth he knew poverty. In adolescence he was an athlete. Restless and determined, he quit school at sixteen to work with his father, digging ditches in New York. He enlisted in the Army at seventeen to make his own way and ended up becoming a paratrooper for the extra sixty dollars a month in jump pay—a lot of money in the mid-1950s. To my knowledge he has never belabored or bemoaned the fact that cancer took his bride at a young age, leaving him alone with an eleven-year-old daughter and a six-year-old son to raise on a carpenter's pay.

My daughter, that baby of seventeen years ago, is going to her senior prom in a few weeks—this I still cannot seem to grasp. Her brothers, fourteen and twelve, are already fine young men. And my bride of eighteen years is more beautiful now than when I fell so completely in love with her in the summer of 1990.

Recently, the five of us were piling into our van to go for ice cream. I went to open the door for my wife, and—not for the first time—one of my boys beat me to it and held the door for his mother. As she got in, his eyes met mine and I nodded my approval. He returned the gesture, a subtle, silent exchange between men that confirmed my belief about character—where it comes from and how it is painstakingly built one example at a time. I felt the heady significance of that legacy handed down from my dad, the same legacy my wife and I will pass along to our children: We are family, and we take care of each other. That's how it goes. You do whatever it takes.

# THE MOST NORMAL THING

PAUL FURTAW

I HAD BEEN OUT OF CONTACT with my father for four years by the time my younger brother called. I had severed ties with the old man because he had been pestering me with nonstop voice mail messages, clinging to me like the kid at recess whom no one wants to play with. My dad was all worked up, but about what, I couldn't decipher. I was determined to stop putting my own success on the back burner, fed up with playing the caregiver instead of the breadwinner, tired of propping up others while I fell short of my own aspirations. So I sent my father a terse e-mail that, in not so many words, let him know I wasn't willing to go down with his ship. At the time, my brother found the note unnecessarily harsh. I didn't know that my dad, though not yet seventy, had long since embarked on his steady decline.

Then came the call from little bro to tell me something was up and that he could use some help with Fran (or Francis, as he'd taken to calling himself since absconding for the West Coast with the burden of child-support payments weighing on him and having exhausted all his opportunities to reinvent himself back East). Apparently our father and his new sweetheart, Elsie, had reached out to advise my brother that things weren't quite right with Dad's health, despite his long-stated plans to live forever. Francis was having trouble with his memory, and he was acting oddly. Elsie suggested we might want to get involved because, after all, he was our father.

As I came on the scene, my father—a former marine, naval midshipman, competitive ocean sailor, and deep-sea submariner—was undergoing amino acid replacement treatment and brain wave therapy from a chiropractor who must have fancied himself a New Age amalgam of neurosurgeon and shaman. Instead, I got my father to a geriatric research center at a San Diego medical school, where they offered free evaluations of seniors with memory impairment.

So there we sat, at the faux walnut laminate conference room table, an unapologetic absentee father with his two alienated but nonetheless dutiful sons at his side, the three of us reunited by pragmatic necessity. Elsie was there too, as if to keep all the unfinished business from spontaneously combusting. She knew Francis only as the doting, half-charming, half-loopy, graying older gentleman with whom she had taken up residence. He was wearing his dress-to-impress clothes: a freshly starched and pressed white pinpoint oxford, tight-fitting blue jeans, and newly polished dress shoes.

After the junior members of the treatment team had exchanged pleasantries with us, the lead doctor cut to the chase: My father was losing his faculties.

Dad's mother, Annabelle, had battled dementia, as did her sister, Mary, and their Aunt Hilda. Annabelle had abandoned my father and his little sister while both were still young children so that she could flee a marriage gone sour and the Midwest for the land of promise: Southern California. Still, Dad was the one who took the lead with placing these three women in nursing homes as each in turn lost the ability to care for herself.

When the doctor told Dad he had dementia, he added that he couldn't be sure of the type, given the variety of insults to my father's gray matter: too much liquor, boxing blows, other assorted traumatic brain injuries, and bad genes. The doctor said it would be in everyone's best interests if he did not drive again. This he told to a man who, when life confronted him with a challenge, would simply load up his car—early on with a wife and three kids, later with various animal companions, and eventually with no more than his sailor's trunk full of clothes and the paper proof of his travails—and drive away. In this way, he had been able to outdistance every problem that had ever threatened to bring him to a standstill.

Dad took the news hard; in fact, he teared up, but he didn't cry. He complimented the doctor and the team on their expertise and their generosity with their time, as if he, the ever-class-conscious son of a caretaker on an estate in Grosse Pointe Farms, Michigan, was not worthy of their efforts. I rubbed his back as I sat beside him, not sure whether it made him more or less anxious, but needing to distract myself from having to watch him squirm inside his own skin. His eyes betrayed that he was wrestling with the knowledge that he had just received his death sentence.

As the weeks and months passed, the man I called Dad steadily disappeared down a very long tunnel. Like so many people with dementia, he periodically would manage to rally and reemerge, as if to say, "What's wrong here? I'm giving this the fight of my life, but it's not working." He went from being six foot three and more than 225 pounds to not much more than skin and bones, a shadow of a man, fueled mainly by chocolate milkshakes and delirious daydreams of when he would see his girlfriend next and maybe, just maybe, get to go home with her to stay. And all the while, the strangest goddamn thing was happening: The motherfucker was gaining grace, integrity, and even character by virtue of his will to endure.

I tell those who learn of his recent death and attempt to offer their condolences, "No, don't feel sorry for me. His was a good death. To live longer is what would have been tragic and sorrow-filled. To a person, we are all at peace, I kid you not." For those with fathers who raised them and therefore fathers to grieve, I have to put his death in the context of his life to convey the true impact on me. I explain, a bit too gleefully at first, and then a bit too sheepishly, "Don't you see? It was the most normal thing he ever did for me as a father—the dying, that is—because I had pretty much counted on him outliving me, if only out of spite."

But he did die—believe me, I made sure of it. I held his cold, half-curled hand, stared at his sunken-jawed face, listened for a final raspy breath, but he was no longer there, having skipped town for the very last time. My father's final wish was to be cremated and for his ashes to be scattered at sea. My brother and I, we did that much for him. I note, finally with a son's pride, that we saw him through.

# SKEFF

JOHN SHEEHY

HELENA, JULY 2006

For many years, because he is who he is and I am who I am, I was not
even aware that I never had told my father I love him. I want to tell him
now, but it has taken me weeks to get around to it—mulling it over,
thinking about when the right time would be, about how it should be
said, with what kind of look on my face and what kind of posture. I
want to say it so it stays said. I want it to be final.

I have put it off until the last minute of this trip home to Helena,
Montana, until this morning, as I am about to get on a plane. Dad and I
got up early and had coffee in the kitchen while Rita, my mom, got ready
to go to the Y for her swim. I picked up my bag and put it in the back of
Dad's car. Then I came back into the house to say good-bye to Mom. We

hugged and got a little misty, Mom and I, said how glad we were to see each other, and then pulled away from each other. As I moved toward the door Mom stood behind me, silent, watching me go.

Dad drove me to the airport and then came in with me.

It is early, and because of the new security rules we can't go to the gate where the seats are, so we hang around on our feet, waiting for my flight to be called. We look at our shoes and chat. I know Dad is happy to be here, happy that I have taken an interest in him, in his history and in Butte, the high-mountain mining town in Montana where he grew up. We talk about his name, about how nobody in Butte ever called anybody by their real name. So, instead of John, he was always Skeff, after the Irish patriot. Somehow he is Skeff more than Dad when he tells me more funny stories about Butte, about his life as a lawyer, about his father, Con. I try to tell some funny stories, too. We are laughing when I hear the voice on the speaker announcing my flight. Time to go. Looking at my shoes, I tell Dad I'd better get moving. He reaches out with his right hand, his good hand. I shake it, and when I pull my hand away there is a fifty-dollar bill in it. "Spend it on Jill," he says. I nod; Jill is my wife. "I will."

As he walks away I think it is now or never. I shout after him. It's louder than I'd planned, more awkward than I'd hoped. "Dad!" I shout. "Dad! I love you!"

He turns only half around, and when he does he stumbles a little bit. For just part of a second, for just long enough for me to register the image, Skeff looks like an old man. But then he doesn't anymore, and he smiles, and he is still smiling and already turning away when he replies, "Thanks."

HELENA, JUNE 2005

I thought I had lost it, had lost it all, when I realized that I'd let the batteries die in the recorder. A whole day with Dad and Mom, that whole day in Anaconda and Butte, in May last year, tramping through all those old gallus frames and all those old memories, gone now, blinked out, no longer held in that magical electrical suspension inside the digital voice recorder.

But I changed the batteries and it was all still there, Mom and

Dad and me and a clear spring day, all safely embedded in a tiny mineral vault of mysteriously etched silicon. I put the earphones in and pressed play, and I can hear it all again.

*In . . . out . . . in . . . out . . . in . . .*

I had missed too much already, lost too much. I am my father's youngest son, the eleventh of eleven children, so it is not my fault that I missed out on most of his life. But it is partly my fault—and, I suppose, partly his, although that hardly matters anymore—that I missed out on so much of the rest.

Now he is eighty-seven, and I am almost forty, and many of the things I thought were important when I was eighteen don't seem important anymore, and many of the things I thought were not, do. I can't quite say what I've missed, but I want to know things. I want to know him if I can, and now, while I can. And, if I can't, I want to know stories, want to know what happened. I want to know about Butte.

I had ridden my bike out to the Wal-Mart in Helena to buy the recorder because I didn't want to miss anything that day, didn't want to miss any more. I had put in fresh batteries and plugged in the throat mike that came with it. Then I put the recorder in the inside pocket of Dad's jacket and clipped the throat mike to his lapel. *There,* I thought. *Now I can't miss anything.*

*In . . . out . . . in . . .*

In the car the mike was useless. Dad said some things here and there, but I can't make them all out now, as I listen with the earphones. The damn mike is too sensitive. It has no judgment. It can't tell the difference between Dad's voice and the noise of the road or the noise a crumpling candy-bar wrapper makes in the front seat. Before I put the recorder in Dad's jacket pocket I had set it to voice-activated mode, so it would turn on only when Dad talked. But as I listen on the earphones I realize that the recorder was on the whole time because it could register Dad breathing. I could hear his ragged, desperate gasps.

*In . . . out . . . in . . . out . . .*

A microphone can't ignore that sound the way I do, the way the family does. And the *Harumpup!* Dad makes every thirty seconds or so when he clears the phlegm out of his throat is so loud I have to take the earphones out of my ears. I listen to the whole recording, all eight hours of it, with the earphones resting on my temples.

On the recording, we are driving a familiar road. They're all familiar roads to Dad, but this one especially so, the sixty miles over the Boulder pass from Helena to Butte that he's driven 5,000 times. We drive through Boulder on the other side of the pass, drive through Basin, drive down from the mountain of my father's old age, back over the hill into the high valley of his boyhood.

Aware of the mike, he plays the tour guide, points to the now-defunct hospital for retarded children in Boulder, remembers for me the story of a case he once had involving a woman who was sent there. "A horrible place," he shudders. "Just an awful place. Poor woman." *Harumpup!*

We're going to Anaconda for a funeral before we go to Butte. So we get off the interstate at the exit with the Racetrack sign. Dad points to the sign and tells me the story about Marcus Daly, one of the copper kings and the founder of the Anaconda Copper Mining Company. He tells about how Daly loved horses and raised his racing stock out here. He tells the story about Daly's favorite horse, Tammany, how back when Daly pretty much owned Anaconda he had a mosaic of Tammany inlaid in the floor of the grand lobby of the town's Montana Hotel. Anybody who stepped on Tammany's head had to buy drinks for the house. "Racetrack," Dad says. "This is where the swells used to go when I was a kid—*Harumpup!*—This is where you went if you wanted to have a big time, get away from Butte."

We drive on toward Anaconda. Dad points out a big sandstone building blooming by itself and out of place on the side of the road at the turnoff to Warm Springs. "That was William Clark's bank there," he says. Clark was another one of the copper kings, Marcus Daly's nemesis and opposite number in every way. He was cool where Daly was warm, acerbic where Daly was funny, angry where Daly was kind, but Irish, too, as Irish as Daly and so fitting with Daly into the pantheon of Butte Irish history." That's where Clark put his money, at least at first. He had too much, too much to trust to anybody else, so he started his own bank to hold it and started making loans, buying the place up. Had one up in Deer Lodge, too, a bigger one, the first one."

For a long space in the recording, then, I can't make out what

Dad is saying. I hear Mom beside him, poking her head up from the crossword, asking an occasional question. For fifteen minutes, though, it's mostly *in . . . out . . . in . . . out . . . Harumpup!*

Long before we reach Anaconda we can see the smokestack. It's still there, even though the smelter's been defunct for almost twenty years. Dad says nothing. He doesn't need to. I can remember him pointing to it when I was a kid, his right hand shaped like a gun as he aimed at it over the steering wheel he held loosely in his broken left hand. "See that?" he said back then. "That's the largest smokestack in the world. Did you know that the *rim* of that stack is wide enough for an airplane to land on? A four-horse team, hitched up side by side, could walk around the rim of that chimney without ever getting close enough to the edge of it to know they weren't right here on the ground. That's something to see, isn't it?"

On the recording I can hear my own voice: "What's that over there, Dad?" We are passing a group of buildings to the right of the road, on the other side of the railroad spur. There are five of them, one big one and four smaller ones around it, all dull red brick and blank concrete. It's an institution of some kind, afloat in an empty parking lot with grass growing in the cracks and saplings growing in the potholes. Many of the windows of the buildings are broken, and the rest are covered with gray road grime or plywood. The front door of the biggest building is chained and padlocked. "Dad? What's that over there?"

He doesn't look. "That?—*Harumpup!*—Oh, that's Galen. I thought you knew that. That was the old TB hospital. That's where Con died."

ANACONDA, MAY 2005

It's not that they don't care. It's just that they've done this so often, have been to so many funerals now, have put so many of their friends and relatives under the ground. They know what it means now, and perhaps what it doesn't; know that their friend, their mother or father, their brother or sister, is not to be sought in the mute limp thing that lies before them in the box, is not to be found behind the slack flesh of what before was a face, on which now is painted a caricature of contrived and eyeless piety.

Skeff and Rita walk up to the casket and look in. Each kneels before it to make a quick and silent prayer. I follow suit—I know the drill, even though I never knew the man—and, as they did, I turn away while still making the sign of the cross. Then the three of us shuffle with folded hands and downcast eyes to the back of the empty room in which the casketed man is almost finished being waked. His funeral will immediately follow the wake.

Skeff and Rita make small talk, sitting sideways in their folding chairs with their arms hung over the plastic backs, looking at their shoes and speaking in low tones of ordinary things: memories, children, grandchildren. Sometimes they laugh, almost silently. Skeff talks about the man in the box and his children, about people he has known in Anaconda, about Anaconda generally. "Tell you what," he says softly, as he sits with his elbows on his knees and his eyes on the floor, "they're famous here for sweet potato pie. When you're in Anaconda, you should always try to get some sweet potato pie." He leans back in his chair and is silent. He watches one of his feet tap absently against the other.

We had pulled into Anaconda about ten that morning and, since we were too early to go to the funeral home, we went for a drive around town. In many ways the town looked the same as the last time I saw it, sometime in the '80s, when the smelter had only just closed and the reality of the Company's abandonment had not yet quite sunk in here or in Butte, either. Anaconda is still overshadowed by the smelter, and the first sign you see of the town is still the stack, that huge brick phallus visible from many miles away, but you fail to realize its true enormity until you're right under it. And still there is the slag, everywhere you look, huge heaps of black burnt rock, twenty and thirty and forty feet high and lined up in serried rows miles long all around the smelter. *This is what's left of Butte that wasn't copper*, I thought.

The buildings were all there, but Anaconda was gone. People were still there, though not anywhere near as many as in the '80s, much less the '40s or '50s, when this town was as bustling as Butte was, and the union jobs at the smelter could give 10,000 families a good living. But the people we saw today looked more like survivors than anything else, like people who managed to live through an apocalypse, people who woke up one day to the stark and simple revelation that their world was no longer there, who woke up one other day not long after that to the more sobering realization that it wasn't coming back. A few of the houses in Anaconda were freshly painted and well kept, but these only served to highlight the sadness of the rest, the houses that seemed to be relaxing entropically into the slag. Like the slag itself, they seemed light and hollowed-out, leeched of what was valuable in them, blackened and slackly and complacently falling apart.

As we drove through town, Skeff pointed in his familiar way—with his hand like a pistol—over the steering wheel or across the dashboard to objects in his memory. "That was where . . ." he said, and "Over there . . ." But what was there and over there were slag piles now, or broken, empty houses, or the shells of beater cars in the yards, or an old man shuffling down the avenue on his way to the bar or to the church or to the funeral. After a while Skeff didn't talk anymore, retreating into his private thoughts behind the ragged sound of his own breathing. Every fifteen minutes or so he took a hit on the inhaler and then cleared his throat. He reached without thinking to the key chain hanging from the dashboard to finger the small rosary on it. In the rearview mirror I could see his lips moving almost imperceptibly: *Hail Mary full of grace.*

"It's an old man's town," he said, out of nowhere. "It wasn't always. But it's an old man's town now."

When the funeral service is over, when the Mass has been said and our Communion taken and the pallbearers have carried the body out to the hearse on the street, we rise with the rest and move toward the doors. A lot of old folks are in the crowd. Rita and Skeff stop to chat with a few of them, to say hi and catch up briefly over handshakes and quiet smiles. There are a few people my age and younger in the crowd, and most of them, like me, are quiet. We are along for the ride, and we maintain a respectful, overly solicitous distance from the old folks and their doings and their dyings. We wait, and the crowd moves us slowly toward the door and out.

"Well," Skeff says, "we'd better get down to the lunch. Better hop-to. There's sure to be a sweet potato pie."

ABSAROKEE, JULY 2005
On the voice recorder I can hear Skeff singing, as he's always done, while

he drives, while he moves, singing those old sentimental songs.

> If you ever go across the sea to Ireland,
> Then maybe at the closing of your day,
> You will sit and watch the moonrise over Claddagh,
> And see the sun go down on Galway Bay.

Skeff's voice is not as strong as it once was. Some of the high notes are too high for him, and there's a breathiness now, a tremor, an uncertainty that wasn't there thirty years ago, when I first remember hearing him sing this song in the front seat of another car driving to or from Butte. Now I have heard it so many times I know all the words and I know what he'll do with it. I know he'll throw a little Bing Crosby vibrato into *Claddagh*, enough to make you stop there and consider the sound of that word, how it sounds like the name of a woman. I know he'll hold the high note on *down* and then load the dice, dip into what he'd call the schmaltz bucket by slowing down dramatically on *Galway Baaay*. And I know he'll sing it again, and again, with different der Bingle flourishes each time, with some *boo-boo-boos* or some comic asides, until he gets tired of the sound of it or picks up another of the 500 tunes in his head.

Sitting at a desk in the family cabin in Absarokee, I set down the headphones but leave the voice recorder on. From the table behind me I can hear his voice rising tinny and false out of the cheap headphone speakers while I dial his number in Helena. I want to talk to him, to check some details. The phone rings and rings, and then he picks up, and for a moment I am confused by the double sound of his voice in the here and now on the phone and behind me, singing, in the past. But that passes in a second, and we talk. He sounds happy to hear from me, happy to talk more about Butte, about the old days.

Out of the headphones, faintly, I can hear him starting "Melancholy Baby." His voice is sweet and sad and slow.

> You shouldn't grieve; try and believe
> Life is always sunshine when the heart beats true.
> Be of good cheer, smile through your tears,
> When you're sad it makes me feel the same as you.

I ask him if he remembers the name of the guy who held his hand on after the accident. "Yeah, sure, it was Mutt Lowney," he says.

"Mutt?" I ask. "What was his real name? Do you remember?"

As far as he knows, Mutt was his real name. That's what everybody called him. "Saved my life," he says, "I suppose."

I ask him again about Anna, his mother. What year did she come to Butte? "Nineteen fourteen," he says. He tells me about her sister, his Aunt Kate, who had come out before Anna and prepared the way for them, for Anna and then her younger sister, Nora. "Nora's the one married a Radamaker in Butte," he says. "You know the Radamakers, all the Radamakers, they're all your second cousins." I remember meeting a few Radamakers over the years, at weddings and funerals, but I can't put a face to any of them. I write the name down, try to remember it. I'm starting to feel a little lost.

On the voice recorder I hear the old big finish.

Every cloud must have a silver lining,
Wait until the sun shines through.
Smile, my honey dear, while I kiss away each tear,
Or else I shall be melancholy too.

Dad tells me the story again about how on the day Anna arrived the miners' union hall was blown up, how Frankie Curran, the mayor, had come to the hall in the evening to find it already full of drunk and angry miners talking strike, how Frankie Curran pled for calm, how one of the miners said, "Go to hell," as a warning, maybe, and then the bunch of them threw Frankie Curran out the second-story window. For the next twenty-four hours, Dad says, the miners ran wild, drinking, running through the streets, swearing at each other, shooting at each other, killing each other. They stole the safe out of the union house and one of them poured a bottle of nitroglycerin on it. Turned out the bottle was full of only whiskey, so they had to settle for just plain dynamite. They missed the whiskey, though, after.

In the morning a wide-eyed Anna looked out over the smoking hill, smelled the black powder and the cordite in the air, and asked her sister Kate, "Ah, Lord, is't always like this here?"

Behind me his voice breaks into a swing pace with a familiar laugh in it.

Shape like a melon and a face like a collie!
Oh, come to me my melon-collie baby!

On the phone they come out of him again, the old stories, all the bits and pieces of him and the times before him, all connected but all random, all in pieces still.

He tells me in an aside, almost, that Con lost his eye in the mine before Dad was born. I am surprised nobody ever told me this, that it never came up before. I can almost hear Dad shrug his shoulders on the other end of the line. What's there to say about a lost eye? Or a lost hand, even if it was his own left hand he almost lost in a car accident when he was eighteen. *Well, this is the way it'll be now. Now this is the way it will be.* Why talk about it?

As Dad talks to me I think of him in Butte, as a boy and as an old man, visiting, of his days there growing up somehow overlapping with the days we used to spend at ball games when I was a boy, the day we spent in Butte last spring remembering, like three photographs of the same face all superimposed on each other. I remember how he knew everybody in Butte, always, and everybody still seemed to know him. "How sh'go?" they'd say to each other, and "Good 'n' you?" back. "Tap 'er light," they'd say when they meant good-bye.

Dad tells me funny stories on the phone. He'd tell me only funny ones if he could, I suppose. Maybe he thinks that's all I want to hear, or maybe that's really how it was for him, mostly funny, mostly fun. He tells me how when Con ran for county coroner in 1938 the polls showed he got all the votes in their Virginia Street precinct but four. He tells me how, afterward, Anna sat at the kitchen table poring over the tally, saying under her breath over and over again, "I wonder who the thraithors were?"

We talk for a while about their brogues, about Irish, the sound of it. I ask him why he thinks he doesn't have one and he says he's not sure. "I'm American, I guess. But Mom and Dad talked Irish all the time at home, and those words, you know, they stick with me. I still remember those words, the sound of them. That's still part of me."

Dad says, like it just hit him, that Con even spoke Irish to him on the day he died. "He asked me to light his pipe for him," he says. "That was something I always did for him, something between us, you know. He was lying in that room in Galen, you know, where they'd moved him in the last days, and he was pretty far gone. Couldn't breathe at all. Wasted away. I didn't know it would be his last day, the last time I'd talk to him. You know, how can you know something like that? You don't. You can't. And so the last thing he ever asked me to do, he said to me, 'John'—you know, he called me John there, nobody ever called me John—he said, 'John, will you light my dudeen for me?'"

There's a long silence on the phone. I can hear him breathing. "Did you light it, Dad?"

"No. No, I didn't. I wonder why sometimes. But, you know, I was young then, and I was trying to do what was right, and now, sure, I look back on it, I might have done something different. But then I just said, 'Dad, the doctors here say you can't smoke. Say it's bad for you.'

"You know what he said to me?" He pauses. I think I hear a sound that might be him laughing, might be him crying. "You know what he said? He said, 'I had a cow in the old country had more sense than those doctors.'" We laugh, or make a noise that sounds like laughing. Then a silence unfolds in which I can think of no more to ask him and he of no more stories to tell, so we wrap up quickly. *Goodbye, now. Tap 'er light.*

As I hang up the phone I can hear the voice recorder coming back to life after a long silence in the car. Emerging from those tinny speakers is the familiar sound of an old sentimental song.

> On her back there was tattoo'd a map of Ireland,
> And when she took her bath on Saturday,
> How I loved to watch her soap up over Claddagh
> And watch the suds roll down on Galway Bay!

Skeff always did hate that schmaltz bucket.

BUTTE, MAY 2005

"Did you ever work here, Dad, in the mines?"

"No," Skeff says. "Not me. My dad did, Con did, for most of his life, except those four years he was the county coroner. Lost his left eye down there at some point. Bit broke and a piece of steel flew off and got him in the eye. But when he got too sick, too tired, you know, to go down in the shaft anymore, they still kept him on. But I think the gaffers he knew always had a soft job for him, like some kind of watchman or something like that."

We walk around the mine shaft, poking at things. The ground is littered with the detritus of the work: thickly rusted pieces of heavy machined steel, square-top timbers soaked in creosote and blue with age, old ore cars rusted into orange-black lace, crusted sections of small-gauge track piled waist high, steam shovels, backhoe buckets, and broken bits from the buzzies scattered about. We poke into the blacksmith shop. It's still open and the tools are still there. The dull bits, thick with rust, are still lined up by the grinder for sharpening, as if this were only a holiday and the work might begin again in the morning, when the men return from the Mint Bar, or from the old M&M, where the doors never closed. But the M&M is closed now and for good, and the men will not return today, to the shop nor to the sill station nor to the hoist house behind the gallus frame, which still echoes with their absence.

It's hard to believe when you stand here that they were only men. *They should have been giants*, I think. *This is the architecture of giants.* Everything is huge and heavy. In the hoist house, 4,000 feet of cable as thick as a big man's leg is spooled like thread on a drum reel twenty-five feet in diameter. Behind the reel is a slate board with a giant clock hand on it, pointing at the names of the stops in the shaft scrawled in chalk by the hand of some miner now long gone.

Skeff fingers a piece of metal lying on a dusty, oil-soaked workbench. He tells me two of his older brothers might have worked in the mines a few summers before the war. "My mother didn't want us doing this kind of work. She wanted more." He pauses. "And anyway, when I broke my hand, I was eighteen, and my hand was no good after that, for that kind of work. That was the end of that for me. The end of this. So I went to college."

Skeff watched his father, Con, die, slow and gasping. In the same year he watched his mother, Anna, die. An eldest son expects to see his parents die. But he did not expect to watch as his little brother Joe followed Con some years later, fighting for air the same way and even in the same house, only in Joe's case with a little oxygen bottle on wheels pathetically trailing behind him. But even with the aid of that bottle, Joe's circle, like Con's, narrowed first to the street, then to the yard, then to the house, then to the bed, and then nowhere.

And then Skeff had to watch again, this time in his mind's eye and from a distance but without ever looking away, as Sister Serena, his kid sister and a nun now, stepped off a plane on her way from somewhere to somewhere else, took a cab to one of her own hospitals complaining of a pain in her back she assumed was from riding the airplane so long and so often. Within two weeks Serena, who never smoked in her life, who never strayed from the vows she took at sixteen to remain pure in body and soul, and who never left the hospital once she entered it, died alone, gasping in another iron bed, far from Butte, far from home. The doctors wondered how—in so short a time and with no apparent cause—such a woman could have formed in her lungs the grapefruit-size tumor that killed her.

Maybe Skeff wondered then what kind of poison had been passed to his family along with and within Butte's edenic fruit. They lived twenty-six miles away and usually downwind from what for seventy years was the largest smelter in the world, which was always in operation. In the fields around the smelter's slag heaps sheep for years had quietly died, their loss quietly recompensed by the Company and just as quietly forgotten by the Montana press the Company indirectly owned. He might have wondered what gas, which of the chemicals—radon, arsenic, mercury, copper, lead, sulfur, or something else or all of them in combination—had trickled into *his* water, had rained down from *his* sky, had risen somehow through ore and rock and topsoil or had vented through the still-open shaft without being seen, heard, or smelled.

He might have wondered, but either his lawyer's mind quickly figured the percentages and then saw no further purpose in wondering, or he simply accepted it all without regret. *Well, this is how it will be now. Now this is the way it will be.*

And he maintained that composure and maintains it still. He maintained it even on the day thirty years ago when he was arguing a case before a judge in some small town on the high line and realized, in midsentence, that he couldn't catch his breath, just *couldn't breathe.* He had to ask for a recess. And he saw in that first moment all that would follow, saw the end of his career as a litigating lawyer, the end of the profession on which he had banked his life, the end of arguing cases, the end of defending the weak against the strong, the end of a life he had come to love. And he saw the end, perhaps, of his own special dispensation, his own destiny now revealed to be the same as Con's and Joe's and Sister Serena's, and life revealed to be not just something you die of but something that kills you.

Like Con, he went from doctor to doctor, but none of them could even identify the problem, much less lie about it, much less alleviate it. So within a month of that day in the courtroom it would be impossible for him to play handball anymore, within a year impossible to practice law as a litigator, and within two years impossible to walk more than a mile. He became a judge then, and a good one, but his soul still belonged to litigation, his heart to Butte, and his lungs to Anaconda. His success, as his success always has, only further divided him from himself.

After that he could not even sleep at night, since every time he lay on his back his lungs would fill with fluid and he would wake up coughing, drowning. He gave up on sleeping at night and napped instead, fitfully, in a straight-backed chair, slumped over Shakespeare and the Bible. And he padded around the house in the dark, coughing and spitting up hard balls of phlegm.

Today, at ninety, although drugs have helped him some, he knows that this, this slow drowning, the withering and the incapacity and the shame and the sputum and the mucus, is indeed how it will be now, that this kind of dying, his father's kind of dying, is the price he has been asked to pay for living long enough, for being blessed or cursed or both enough, to have witnessed and given shape to this particular series of accidents, to have watched and listened and flown in those long wheeling concentric circles with Butte at their center.

And he knows, and I know, too, that it will kill him, this thing, that Butte will kill him. It will kill him eventually, and sooner than either of us would like, since neither of us knows how to open ourselves to the other, and both of us know that when he dies so also will Con and Anna and Ireland and Butte, and this time probably for good.

Behind him Skeff will leave eleven children, among them a son who bears a name that was his own, the name by which he will be called again only on the marker of his grave.

# GOD OF MY FATHER

**BRUCE ELLMAN**

I'M RUNNING LATE, as usual. "Leave your BlackBerry in the car," I remind myself while searching for a parking space. I rummage through the center console for a *kippah*, smash it on my head, and run into the synagogue. The service has already begun; I'm relieved that I won't have to endure the entire thing. But I can't miss the end.

. . . .

I'm told that my dad had a good time with his kids. He took the six of us horseback riding and sledding, and he let us bury him in the sand. That's what Mom said. That's what we've watched once every decade or so in the eight-millimeter movies. But I have practically no memories of my father before I reached age ten, only of him gently rubbing my back as I lay in bed, inches from sleep. He would softly sing "Sonny Boy" to me: "When there are gray skies, I don't mind the gray skies. You make them blue, Sonny Boy." To this day, I can't be touched enough. I never wanted him to stop; I always hungered for more.

Dad wanted more, too: a real family, financial security, and power. Only days after he was born, his mother died from delivering her child. Dad had no siblings, a fragile web of relatives, and a father so unprepared to raise a child that he sent his son to the local orphanage for a brief period of time.

Even from this chaotic beginning, Dad still was able to earn a law degree by age twenty-one, marry a beautiful woman, have six healthy children, and forge a stellar career engineering unique and convoluted systems for preserving his clients' wealth.

Dad's college friends described him to me as "brilliant," "driven," and "competitive," the consummate salesman who wouldn't take no for an answer. One of these friends remarked, "When you visit the cemetery, don't be surprised when you see a phone antenna sticking out of the grave. That will be Ed making some calls, trying to sell someone something."

Relentless. That was my father, and tortuously complex. No one could confuse his clients—or save them taxes—like my father could. If he wanted to give you a dollar, he would instead give you a dollar fifty and ask that you loan him back seventy-five cents. But don't worry: He would accrue the interest in arrears, swap the rate, and let you take the tax deduction. So in actuality, you would get the value of two dollars over a twenty-year period.

By age thirty-five, Dad had won the envy and respect of his community for his spectacular professional ascent and for his dedication to philanthropic causes, particularly Jewish ones. Friends and admirers surrounded Dad, yet in a way, he remained as isolated as he was in childhood.

Effective as he was with his business and his charitable organizations, Dad struggled with sharing power. His company was filled with support staff, but he had no potential partners. His most capable, ambitious employees, even his own sons, eventually left the business or were fired. Negotiating control, whether it was with a business associate or a child, proved painfully difficult for Dad. He was best by himself.

· · · ·

Ten people, many of them familiar to me, are already in the chapel when I enter. Jewish law requires a minimum of ten adults for communal prayer, so they were able to start without me, thank God. I find the right page in the *siddur* and join the men and women as they chant, "You are blessed, O Lord, God of Abraham, God of Isaac, God of Jacob . . . God of my father." My praying sounds almost robotic. I try to put the day's events out of my mind so that I can concentrate on my dialogue with God.

· · · ·

In preparation for my Bar Mitzvah, Dad and I went to synagogue on Shabbat morning. If you had ever met my father, you might have assumed he was a very observant Jew. He was always reading from his impressive library of Jewish texts and studying the Talmud, often with an Orthodox rabbi. And he relished observing even the most obscure Jewish fast days.

Yet he maintained only what he called a "kosher-style" home, and on Shabbat he engaged in such prohibited activities as driving his car, spending money, and using electricity. Generally, we were revolving-door Jews, attending synagogue two or three times a year, for only the most important holidays. But my big day was coming, and I had to learn the service. So in the year leading up to my thirteenth birthday, we went to synagogue every Saturday morning. I endured the proceedings, usually while playing with the fringes of my father's *tallit*. "Follow the Hebrew," he would admonish me in a hushed voice. His breath was noxious, a side effect, I later realized, of his antidepressants.

Wrapping my fingers in the long strands of his black-striped cream wool shawl, I could feel his body sway back and forth. I made patterns across my fingers with these fringes and anxiously awaited my reward for sitting patiently. After the service, we would have lunch at the local deli, just Dad and me: chopped liver on bagels. And on the way home, he would let me drive his Lincoln Continental up the driveway.

Soon I would dread being alone with him in that car. That's the place he tried to have "the talk" with me, after I had walked into the bedroom while he and my mother were having sex. We were in the Lincoln on the way to play tennis, one of the few activities we enjoyed together. He nervously tried to engage me in a discussion of what I had witnessed. I squirmed in embarrassment as he stumbled though euphemistic explanations of sex. The only response I could muster was a hasty "I know, I know." I now understand that the experience was as unbearable for him as it was for me.

It was hard for Dad and me to connect. The day I got into Brown University, I was also named as a finalist for my high school's most prestigious graduation award: Head Boy. Bursting with pride, I told him the news. He responded, "I hope you appreciate this day, because in life you often don't get what you want."

Though he celebrated every victory and accomplishment with me, his joy was tucked away, far from reach. Despite his generosity, Dad demonstrated reserve, both emotional and financial. His frugality was legendary and, at times, perplexing. He had a 35,000-square-foot home, but he would drive only used cars (he bought that 1968 Lincoln in 1972), and he preferred to reuse dental floss. Family apocrypha has it that even his toilet paper was not always fresh.

In college, I received a copy of his favorite book, *The Denial of Death*. He bought it by the case and handed out copies as though they were party favors. He valued suffering; it was character-building.

I called him one night from college, in a teary panic. I was studying for my economics final and realized I didn't understand much of anything. When I began sobbing, he gave me a valuable piece of advice: Learn the hell out of a small section of the material. But his compassion was more striking and meaningful than his counsel. Only when I was in utter despair could he connect with me.

．．．．

Voices swirl around me in unison, a chorus of vaguely discernible mumblings: "May His great name grow exalted and sanctified." I sway with the rhythms known to generations of Eastern European Jews and pull gently at the fringed garment around my shoulders, contemplating God's kindness, eternity, mercy, and unity. How can I come to know God? And how do I reconcile His power with my suffering? God of Abraham, God of Isaac, God of Jacob, God of my father, how can You really love me? Why can't I get close to You? Where are You? I ask God the same question God posed to Adam in the garden of perfection, the first question of humanity: "Where are you?" A wave of sadness and despair envelops me.

．．．．

After college, I wandered for fifteen years, geographically, romantically, and professionally. I jetted around the globe for both work and pleasure. Stints with financial powerhouses took me to Asia, Africa, and Latin America. After flirting with international finance, I moved to Los Angeles and tried my hand in the entertainment business, managing talent and running a production company. Dad watched this all with a mixture of pride, confusion, pointed skepticism, hope, concern, anguish, and fickle support.

We fought about his attempts to influence me with money and about my career choices. I bristled at his pontifications and tried to convey my resentment. But I desperately wanted to avoid ending up like my two brothers, both of whom became increasingly alienated from Dad after they resigned from his business.

．．．．

I try to focus on a different prayer each day. My attempts to keep the distractions of work and life from intruding in this holy space are mostly unsuccessful. Despite years of religious school, text study, and a Bar Mitzvah, I'm still fairly clueless as to what all this Hebrew means. The translation provides some hints, but the language is so distant. *Y'hei sh'mei raba m'varakh l'alam ul'al'mei al'maya*: May His great Name be blessed forever and ever.

Do I really love God with all my heart, with all my soul, and with all my might? Is God really my rock and my redeemer?

. . . .

This is what I loved about my father: He tolerated me, tolerated my ranting and confrontations. He knew I was trying to get closer to him, and very few people in his life attempted that. He was receptive to my criticisms, and while he didn't always like them, he took me seriously.

Over time, we found other ways to connect. Dad read his Jewish texts daily, and I, too, began studying scripture and spent several months in Israel engrossed in learning. Dad even came to visit me in Jerusalem. One of my teachers took us to a yeshiva, a traditional place of learning, in the Old City, where pairs and pairs of young, long-bearded men wearing black hats sat at old wooden desks, poring over books and arguing. For a moment, Dad and I became enwrapped in the dialogue that has entranced Jews for thousands of years.

At my wedding, amid the chaos of celebration and transition, Dad and I grabbed each other's arms and spun round and round until the room disappeared. We were locked in an unshakable gaze of delight, fear, and love—two whirling dervishes about to crash but held together by a powerful bond. I'm not sure if he was euphoric because I was about to marry a beautiful rabbi or because of the tax benefits afforded to clergy. No matter, it was just him and me.

Ten years later, Dad was visiting Los Angeles with my mother, and they were the guests of honor at our Shabbat dinner. Our wedding china shone with its intricate pattern of Art Deco swirls and dots, and garden flowers adorned our table. Our silver candlesticks and the braided challah glowed in the flicker of the candles. As I sang the blessings over the wine and welcomed the Sabbath into our home—just as my father and his father had done for decades—Dad, surrounded by three of his grandchildren, was so touched that tears welled up in his eyes. That I was now a psychologist in a thriving private practice only enhanced his pride and delight.

After many years of chasing money, and those in need of it, I've turned to the world of emotions to make my living and discover a purpose in my life. As a psychologist, I have the privilege of entering and engaging in the private, internal worlds of many fine, complicated individuals. I have sought purpose and refuge in intimate relationships where power and control are often shared or at least negotiated. Yet, as Dad was, I am frequently and ultimately alone in my work.

. . . .

We are coming to the final prayers. It's the big finish. It's the reason I'm here. The prayer I've heard thousands of times. Only now, I'm the one saying it. I'm the one standing, publicly announcing my state of despair and loss. Others sit, but I stand and recite the Mourner's Kaddish as I have done every day since my father's collapse. This ancient Aramaic poem, recited daily for eleven months after the death of a parent, does not mention death, sorrow, or loss, only God's greatness:

> May His great Name grow exalted and sanctified in the world that He created as He willed. May He give reign to His kingship in your lifetimes and in your days and in the lifetimes of the entire Family of Israel, swiftly and soon.
>
> May His great Name be blessed forever and ever. Blessed, praised, glorified, exalted, extolled, mighty, upraised, and lauded be the Name of the Holy One. Blessed is He beyond any blessing and song, praise and consolation that are uttered in the world.
>
> May there be abundant peace from Heaven, and life upon us and upon all Israel. He Who makes peace in His heights, may He make peace upon us and upon all Israel.

. . . .

At seventy-five, Dad was fit, trim, mentally keen, professionally engaged, and almost obsessed with his diet and nutritional supplements. "He wasn't the kind of guy to die," I told a friend. My father's existence offered me a sense of comfort and security, and with his death I am confronted with my own aloneness and with the continual pursuit of finding meaning in my life.

I understand that life must go on and the community must move forward, but I'm in agony. It has been seven months since Dad died, and God isn't great and I have not yet found peace or anything close to it. But I understand that my prayers are not only for the sake of tradition, not only out of meaning and respect for my father; they are a means of seeking closeness—closeness with God, and closeness with my father's memory, closeness so that I am not so utterly alone.

I can now recite the Kaddish from memory. My father's black-striped *tallit* gently embraces my shoulders, draping across my heart. I twist and twirl the fringes of his garment around my fingers and reflect upon what he taught me.

He was right: Pain is indispensable to growth. And his death made it clear that we do not have forever to make our lives significant. But I am right, too: Meaning is found within the context of relationship.

My father helped me discover my yearning for closeness. Only in his death have I realized how deeply I love him and the enormity of his impact. When I recite Kaddish and listen very carefully, I can feel his touch.

# NEON

**JAMES HOUGHTON**

FURNACES ROARED and presses clanged in the background as a newly formed, sixty-pound glass TV panel rolled onto the light board at Jenny's final-check station. She was not happy.

"Freeman, you motherfucker! Do that again and I'll kick you so hard Louisa will be using a straw to blow you tonight. Are you checking this shit out, J.R.? Just trying to do my job, and this peckerhead keeps missing blisters the size of Doug's dick!"

I gave my best "Don't-I-know-it-and-I'll-be-watching-you-all" shake of the head—meant to convey both authority and easy familiarity, neither of which I felt—and wandered off to check on the other three assembly lines. I was twenty-nine years old and nine months into a yearlong assignment as a quality-control supervisor on the midnight shift at a television-glass factory in State College, Pennsylvania. I checked my watch—only five minutes had passed since the last time I had looked—and geared myself for another long night of monotonous rounds along the endless factory corridors.

A pair of gloves wrapped in a ball of duct tape whizzed by my head. "Gloveball" was a popular way to relieve boredom on the shift. Did they like me? Were they trying to play with me? Or were they pushing me? Did I need to make an example of someone? A cackle from the loudspeaker spared me from my indecision and called me to the phone.

"Houghton!" I shouted above the din of the presses, relieved to be taken out of the mind-numbing routine and hoping for some shipping crisis that would keep me in the warehouse all night.

"James? This is John Reyman up in Corning." John was a senior executive and a good friend of my father's. He was also my unofficial mentor, tasked with making sure my career was moving in the right direction. "We think everything is going to be OK, but your dad has just been in an accident and he's being taken to a hospital in Virginia. We're sending your mom down on a plane, and we're going to stop and pick you up in an hour. We just think it would be best if you were all together right now."

My first reaction was relief: I was exhausted after six days on the midnight shift, and getting out a day early seemed like a gift.

"Thanks, John. I appreciate the call. Are you really sure I need to go down? What kind of accident? What do you mean you *think* everything is going to be okay?"

"Well . . ." My stomach sank. "We don't really have all the details yet and won't really know until he gets to the trauma center in Norfolk. He was hit by a car and was pretty banged up. The good news is that he's stable and being helicoptered to Norfolk as we speak. I think your mom could really use you right now."

An hour later I was standing alone on the tarmac at the local airport, the glare of two street lamps overhead acting as a beacon for the slowly approaching Falcon jet. The engines screamed one final time as the plane rolled to a stop. Mom was silhouetted through one of the porthole windows, waving with false bravado. The door hissed open and the steps unfurled to the ground. Bob Simon, one of the pilots, made his way down the stairs and shook my hand grimly. I muttered my greetings and thanks and launched up the steps into the familiar, beige-and-leather confines of the tube. "Hi, Mom. Is everything going to be OK?"

. . . .

My father, Jamie Houghton, was the CEO of Corning Inc., a glass manufacturing company started by his great-great-grandfather, Amory Houghton, in Somerville, Massachusetts, in 1851. In 1868, after a brief stop in Brooklyn, New York, Amory floated his whole operation via the Erie Canal to the banks of the Chemung River and the town of Corning in western New York. From this humble start the company had grown significantly. Corning now had more than 25,000 employees around the world and was known for such consumer brands as CorningWare, Pyrex, and Steuben, as well as for the fundamental research that led to such world-changing technologies as the glass lightbulb, the envelope for the cathode-ray tube (which enabled the mass adoption of the television), and fiber optics.

Though the company had gone public in the 1940s, four decades before he became CEO, Dad was the sixth Houghton to run Corning. He had taken over from his brother, who had taken over from their father, who had taken over from his father, and so on. Not all the transitions had been smooth. My great-grandfather, Alanson B. Houghton, a bookish intellectual and the first in the family to go to Harvard, had his heart set on a career in academia but was forced to return from his graduate studies in Germany to take over the business during a severe recession in the late 1800s. Whatever his personal misgivings, he lived up to his responsibility well. He not only saved the company, he significantly increased its size over the next twenty years.

Alanson eventually heeded the call of public service and became a U.S. congressman. In 1922, he was appointed as the U.S. ambassador to Germany (and later Great Britain), leaving his twenty-one-year-old son, my grandfather Amory, behind to look after the family business. After a few years under the tutelage of some more senior executives, my grandfather ran the company successfully for thirty-five years, before he too was named an ambassador, to France. He was followed by his eldest son, my uncle Amo, who ran Corning and continued to grow it until 1983, when, during a particularly difficult period for the business, he turned the reins over to his brother, my father. A few years later, Amo was elected as the U.S. congressman for our district.

When Dad took over he was forty-eight years old and a well-liked if not entirely proven commodity. Ten years later, when I started my shifts in the television-glass factory, Corning was prosperous once again and Dad had recently been on the cover of *BusinessWeek*.

· · · ·

I grew up in Corning, the rural factory town where most of the 12,000 residents had a family member who worked for the company and where everyone knew my name. I also grew up with the Corning company lore and with the tradition of a family that was recognized for its business skills and for its commitment to service and the community. The experience was both exhilarating and inhibiting.

Even at a young age I felt the tension between my intense pride in the company and in my family and a great longing to be anonymous. I adored my father and grandfather and uncle; nothing made me happier than skipping through the local museum with visiting friends and casually pointing out their names on plaques and signposts recognizing their role in the town and company histories. Whenever we traveled I made a big show of turning over dinner plates or teacups to make sure that they carried the Corning logo. And I was not immune to the thrill of flying on the company plane, being whisked away in a limousine when we landed, and staying in five-star hotels wherever we went.

But I also was embarrassed by the attention I received. I became hypersensitive to our last name. I prayed that teachers would not call out "Houghton" when taking attendance. I worried that friends wanted to play with me only because I was a Houghton. I even insisted to bullies on the playground that my name was Richard Smith. I would lie on the floor of my dad's Mercedes when we drove around town and would beg my parents to drop me off three blocks from school so that no one would see me get out of the car. I rarely asked other kids over to play, fearing their reaction to our large, modern house; my fantasy was to live as my best friend did, in a cramped, three-bedroom ranch with five siblings and a TV in the kitchen.

Relief and relative anonymity came when I was shipped off to boarding school after ninth grade. Three generations of our family had preceded me there, but in many ways I was just another rich kid. No one cared about my name or family history, and I was free to succeed or fail on my own merits, with no more self-consciousness than any other teenager. I thrived there. I was especially drawn to the theater and made a modest name for myself as an actor and director. While I loved the applause and recognition, I also relished the independence and valida- tion the theater provided; I was good at something that had nothing to do with my last name. I began to dream about breaking the family tradition of working for Corning and becoming an actor instead.

For all the newfound freedom of boarding school, for all the excite- ment I felt about the possibility of being different from the rest of my family, in reality my return to Corning began even before I had left. I was seduced by the stories of my ancestors' good deeds, by the pride I felt in the products that the company made, and by the reverence and deference with which our family was treated (even if it occasionally came with unwanted attention). And there also was unintended but powerful grooming. My father would occasionally take either my sister or me with him on business trips to South America, Eastern Europe, or Asia. Despite the agony of being pulled out of school and having to explain to friends where I was going, these were magical times. I loved the exotic travel and the special attention we received at each destina- tion, and these trips also gave me time alone with Dad.

We would spend many hours on the plane, talking about every- thing from baseball to fishing to school. But the conversations became truly interesting when we talked about the company, the reason for the trip, the role Dad was playing, his confidential assessment of various managers and partners who we would meet. His pride and enthusiasm for his job were infectious, and he would inevitably share how happy he would be if I wanted to work for the company someday. He never made it an explicit expectation, and he was always careful to say that I could do whatever I wanted, but he would invariably share his bias.

"You should know," he would say in the cozy confidence I came to crave, "you are a great guy and I know that you would be great at this. People really like being around you—and that's what this is all about: people skills." The hook was set in those moments. Flying at 35,000 feet, in first class, on our way to Japan or Poland or Indonesia, with the embrace of my father's proud approval, I found it hard not to resist the idea of the shiny brass ring that Corning represented.

. . . .

My grand plans for rebellion, hatched at boarding school, began with the decision to apply for early acceptance to Brown, instead of Harvard, where three generations of my family and many of my cousins had gone before me. The insurrection sputtered out three months later when I sheepishly realized that maybe I was just acting out of spite and that perhaps it made sense to have more of a choice after all. I entered Harvard that fall.

This pattern of dipping my toe into less familiar water before inevitably pursuing a more familiar route would persist for many years. At Harvard I continued to act and enjoyed hanging out with the drama crowd, but I also followed my father's footsteps as president of an exclusive all-male social club. My romantic notion of spending a summer immersed in French culture was ultimately made possible by my taking a job in a Corning factory south of Paris. After graduation I spent a year and a half teaching and traveling in Africa and returned intent on working for Save the Children or USAID. But I was swayed by advice, from those in the field, that to be really effective in the nonprofit world I needed more practical, for-profit business experience. When my interviews at several management consulting firms fizzled in spectacular displays of ineptitude—I was unable to explain the difference between revenue and profit, let alone estimate the number of AAA batteries sold in America each year—I was rescued by an offer to join the training program of a large investment bank, on whose board my father happened to sit.

Four years after I returned from Africa I found myself in London, twelve lonely months into an expat assignment with the bank and struggling to write applications to graduate school. "Why do you want to go to business school?" the essays demanded. I had no idea. What I did know is that I had spent a long time trying to pursue a different path—partly to prove that I could do something different from what my father and uncle and grandfather had done, partly to hedge my bets and keep my options open as long as possible. The time had come to face the inevitable. I knew that if I did not I would always wonder. It was time to stop resisting. It was time to admit that I wanted to try.

"Dad," I croaked into the phone from London, "who should I talk to if I wanted to learn more about the possibility of coming to work for Corning?"

"That's something to think about," came his careful reply. "I'll set up a call with John Reyman."

· · · ·

The plane landed on the rain-soaked tarmac, and we were soon hurtling through deserted streets to the Norfolk naval hospital. Dad had been airlifted to the trauma center after being struck by a car in Williamsburg, Virginia, some forth-five miles away. He had just finished dinner and was crossing the street back to his hotel when a busboy at the end of his shift drove out of the garage at twenty miles per hour and hit him, throwing him into the air. Dad broke several ribs, shattered his right leg, and suffered a severe blow to his head.

Two surgeons met Mom and me as we entered the disorienting green glare of the emergency room. They explained that the situation was stable for the moment but that they needed to operate immediately. They wanted to put a rod in his tibia, screw the rest of the bones back in place, and insert a shunt to drain excess fluid and relieve pressure on his brain. Mom and I stared dumbly, comforted by their curt competence but neither of us daring to ask the obvious question. We merely nodded our consent to their hurried requests to proceed.

We turned to follow a nurse to a waiting room, and there was Dad. He was being ferried on a stretcher, surrounded by trauma personnel and covered by bandages and tubes. "If you want to talk to him, now's your chance," one of the surgeons offered. "He is going to be out of it for a while."

"Hey Dad," I mumbled weakly, "how are you doing?"

"Hey," he tried to smile back and reached out his hand. "What are you doing here? I am such an idiot. This is just so stupid. You shouldn't have come. I am so sorry to drag you into this. How do I look?"

When he saw Mom he let out a stifled cry and grabbed her hand as hard as he could. "I am so sorry," he said. "I am just so sorry."

· · · ·

The haze that followed over the next twenty-four hours included many hushed consultations, with the doctors and with various company executives who began to assemble to help manage the crisis. Dad had come through the first set of surgeries but was still in intensive care and would require several more operations. Despite their gravity and repeated references to "a major trauma," the surgeons seemed confident that Dad would make it. But it was unclear whether he would suffer any lasting damage. The Corning executives, meanwhile, started planning how to deal with the impact the news could have on the company's stock price and on the broader Corning community. The company may have been on a roll, but now the CEO was gone, and this would be the first time in many years that a Houghton wasn't at the helm. I sensed that the looks of concern directed my way were about more than sympathy.

Sometime the next morning, I got a call from John Reyman. "You know your family means a lot to this community," he blurted after a few minutes. "I think we ought to get you back up from State College. I think people are going to want to see you here. I think people are going to want to know that you are moving up."

My heart jumped. The thought of leaving the swing shift three months earlier than planned had its appeal. "I don't know, John," I hedged. "I just want to be sure that I pay my dues and get as much as I can out of it. I'm not looking for special treatment."

"I'm not talking about special treatment," he barked back. "You did your time and by all accounts, you've done a great job. You've proven you're good with people. You're ready. Folks get transferred all the time.

I'm talking about stepping up. We're going to need you in a more visible role—especially if your Dad isn't around anymore."

The reality and the opportunity hit me hard. For a brief, shining moment the path was clear and my destiny was fulfilled. Just like my great-grandfather and grandfather and father before me, I now had the chance to rise to an unforeseen challenge and step into the role that I was born for. Never mind that the company was ten times bigger than it had been during my grandfather's era, or that I had not the first clue about running a business.

There was no longer time for angst-ridden soul-searching about what I really wanted to do with my life. I was emboldened by the responsibility of helping Dad in a time of need and grateful to be released from the ambivalence I had felt about returning to work for Corning. Here was my real purpose. If the company needed me, I was ready.

The moment did not last long.

. . . .

Dad got better, and John Reyman dropped dead a few months after the accident. John had been a good friend of Dad's, a local-born consigliere who cared deeply about the company and the town and our family. Dad took John's death hard. He had relied on him for his loyalty and candor and his uncanny feel for the pulse of the company. He also had asked John to look after me.

I did move up from State College, back to Corning and into a midlevel marketing job in the new division that made the flat glass for LCD screens. With Dad on the mend and John Reyman gone, the urgency to get me into a more visible leadership role faded; my new mentors seemed content to let me earn my way up the old-fashioned way.

Over the next four years I worked hard to prove myself. After a year of helping to develop a new LCD product, I was given my own business to run, one that made a line of components for traditional TVs. It was a small operation, but I had my own direct reports, accountability for profit and loss, customers all over the world, and indirect responsibility for 150 manufacturing jobs. It was the ideal environment to test my aptitude and passion for business. And yet, while the business grew and the feedback I received was positive, doubts began to emerge. Not only was I hard on myself, beating myself up for not understanding every aspect of the business or handling every situation perfectly, but I started questioning the validity of the feedback. Did they really mean what they said, or were they just saying it because I was Jamie's son?

I had many long, heartfelt talks with Dad and would confide my doubts about my ability and my passion and my long-term future at Corning. Dad would listen sympathetically, acknowledging that he too had doubts at my age, that his nickname in college had been Atlas because he seemed to carry the weight of the world on his shoulders. But he would also tell me he had no doubts about my ability, that he was hearing nothing but great things about my performance and people skills, and that all these current jobs, while perhaps less than stimulating, were the important stepping stones for the years ahead. I always felt better after we talked. His calming assurances would settle me down for a month or two. But as this pattern repeated itself, I began to wonder if my ambivalence and reservations were a result of something more than just our shared tendency to worry. Maybe, I sometimes dared to think, we were just different people. Maybe this was not about my ability but about my desire.

· · · ·

The end came on a moonlit pier in Hong Kong.

My wife, Connie, and I had been sent to Hong Kong on a house-hunting trip, to prepare for my latest promotion and transfer. I had spent the previous year in the division that made optical fiber, the company's fastest-growing and most profitable business. I had been working on a project to develop our overall sales and manufacturing strategy for China and Southeast Asia. The pace had been exhausting. The head of the division, widely acknowledged to be the company's rising star, was determined to succeed in China and drove the team hard. My immediate boss, the company's wiliest deal maker, had become increasingly frustrated with the countless roadblocks being thrown up by the inscrutable Chinese authorities. I was spending at least a week each month in China and the rest of the time back in Corning, attending endless strategy sessions surrounded by legions of McKinsey consultants.

It became clear that we needed a person on the ground in China to help manage the process, and I was offered the position. I was in the midst of another wave of doubt about my future, and I convinced myself that Hong Kong would provide the necessary distance and clarity to assess once and for all whether working for Corning was the right thing for me in the long term.

As we stood on the pier, looking across Victoria Harbour and admiring the cacophony of neon and high-rises and ancient boats set against the distant peaks of mainland China, Connie and I debated the pluses and minuses of the move. It was hard to ignore the energy and excitement of the city, but we had just spent the week looking at sterile corporate apartments and we both had a few reservations about immersing ourselves in an expat community that, while dynamic, still seemed overly enamored with its colonial legacy.

As the lights flickered and danced on the harbor, it struck me that my attraction to this seemingly enchanted city was not unlike my long dance with the allure of Corning. The idea of moving to an exotic locale had held such romantic appeal, until we were confronted with the stark reality of expat life. Perhaps I had been drawn more to the idea of Corning than to the reality of working as a business manager in a large corporation in a small town in upstate New York. People skills and family history and expectations didn't matter; all that mattered was whether I wanted to do the job. And if working in the company's most desirable division, with its best managers, on one of its most high-profile projects did not excite me, then was there any position at Corning that would?

"Well," I muttered, "at least we'll have the experience of being in Asia for a few years. And if it doesn't work out, I can quit, and we can figure it out from there."

"Why are we doing this?" Connie asked. "If you really don't think Corning is for you, why do we need to move 10,000 miles away just to make sure?"

I looked at her without answering. Two days later I called Dad and told him that I was resigning.

# HUSBANDS

# SEX AND DRUGS MADE ME A MAN

JESSE KORNBLUTH

EVERYTHING I KNOW about being a man I learned from women, and especially when we were stoned and in bed, fucking and/or talking.

Men who have reached the AARP age, if my conversations with my brethren are at all typical, do not think this way. We're above sex now—or at least above talking about it. When we take the measure of our lives, we speak *of mentors* and *character* and *hard work*, and if we can stand to offer a reason to explain the good things we've got without beating the drums for our personal excellence, we may even throw in *luck*. Thanking the women who took us into their bodies? When I mention that, guys give me the look that says, "You're weird."

If I were the careful sort, I'd assign sex and drugs to the rock 'n' roll phase of my life—and pretend that phase ended long ago. Because in the Gospel according to Media, life has this arc: When we were children, we acted like children and smoked dope and lay with women whose breasts bounced free and easy under their tie-dyed shirts, but now we are men, and we have put away childish things, and drink Bordeaux to self-medicate and need Viagra to rouse us on those rare nights when we feel the urge to bend one into our wives.

Nonsense.

. . . .

I have always feared the male of my species. And with reason.

Several times, when I was four or five, I would look up the wide stairway of our house in Kansas City and see, behind the gauze curtain on the landing, the shadowy figure of a man. Much later, I learned that he was Carl Austin Hall, the former owner of the house. He had returned because he was broke. He was casing the joint.

My mother did laundry in Hall's old champagne tubs; we were chump change. Another family in our neighborhood was dramatically richer, so Hall kidnapped and killed their six-year-old son before coolly collecting a $600,000 ransom. His arrest soon followed, and, eighty-one days after the murder, his execution.

A few years later, after my family had moved to a Boston suburb, it seemed like a good idea for me to join the Cub Scouts. I was small and bookish, but the members of my pack took to me immediately: They cocked their BB guns, told me to start running, and blasted away. Thus ended my scouting career.

I eventually escaped to one of the most exclusive New England boarding schools. T.S. Eliot went there, as did Bobby Kennedy. The academics thrilled me. But my classmates were, for the most part, a sorry bunch of Old Boston losers for whom school was a low priority; when I volunteered a correct answer, they were likely to pound me in the back.

My response to a decade in the company of my gender?

An all-consuming desire for revenge, disguised as ruthless ambition. Global success and massive wealth, yeah, that would show them. So I not only got into Harvard, I skipped my freshman year. Having written my senior thesis in what should have been my junior year, I wisely decided to stick around for a fourth year—our government was on such a rampage that a thousand Americans a month were coming home in body bags from Vietnam—which is how I came to be the first member of the Harvard Class of '68 to publish a book.

Then I ran out of visible targets, and I had no mentors to suggest that creative work could come from an inspiration other than "I'll show them." At twenty-two, I had hit the wall. I had no idea what to do next.

. . . .

Fortunately, from the beginning, there were girls.

At the age of eight, I published a book review in the local newspaper, which was for me what scoring a winning touchdown might have been for another kid. Girls noticed—smart girls, anyway. So I kept at it. Soon my best friends were theatrical girls, girls who wrote poetry, girls overlooked by the football captain and student council president. But a peck on the cheek was the most they gave me; as late as the ninth grade at my suburban junior high school, girls wore full girdles on dates.

Boarding school was a revelation. Just like me, the rich girls had libidos that revved high. I joined every extracurricular activity that involved my mouth. And after the debate and the drama rehearsal and the yearbook meeting, there was likely to be a make-out session that left me wanting more.

In college, the dorms had rules that limited female visitation, so I moved off-campus. The revels commenced promptly. Weekend evenings assumed a pleasant pattern: jug wine, Mexican weed, "Going Home" by the Stones or "Eight Miles High" by the Byrds on the turntable. I never needed to lunge. Long before the room started spinning, we'd be reaching for one another.

There was a war on, and that heightened the urgency of my liaisons. There was an antiwar as well, and the saying had it that girls say yes to guys who say no. Because I was saying no to the government and its filthy war as often and as publicly as possible, many college women said yes to me; they said yes, yes, yes! After a while, I couldn't remember how many women I'd slept with or even that much-cooler statistic, the number of consecutive days I'd gone from one to another.

Desire and war make a recipe for hot, frenzied sex—but not intimacy. In my late teens and early twenties, intimacy was beyond me; my needs were too urgent, too desperate. It had to be obvious to the women I was seeing then that they were a haven for me, shelter from the storm. Maybe that was enough. Maybe I was a haven for them as well.

Still, those early couplings were important preparation for what was to come. And I don't just mean deeper connections; I mean loftier highs: peyote, LSD, and mescaline. These drugs gave deeper sensation, purer flashes. They also generated hours of consciousness. When you took them, you couldn't have sex and then collapse like a drunk into heavy sleep. You had to either get up and go out or talk. I chose to talk.

I can't remember these conversations, but I know that my lovers and I would exchange ideas and swap stories. And I clearly recall that I would listen to these women and take them seriously and accept them as a being as hopeful and as damaged and as scared as I was.

Soon I was feeling quite the adult. Then came spring 1969.

. . . .

Janet (not her real name) was a friend of the sister of a sometime girl-friend. The connection was a little close for comfort, but that sort of thing happened a lot back then. We had a relationship that couldn't have been simpler: When we saw one another, we ripped off our clothes.

Ours was an understandable attraction. I was short, intense, Jewish, and not very interested in outdoor sports. Janet was tall and blonde, with a model's long legs and an athlete's body. We were exact opposites, and we attracted. There was no guilt; we were a romp together, a time out from our lives. Our sex was hot, but innocent. We liked each other a lot, but nothing was at stake.

On the night I'm recalling now—a night I'll cherish until my last breath—Janet was still living in Cambridge, and I'd moved to a communal farm in western Massachusetts. The male-female ratio was wretched there, and the heroic males wore overalls. After weeks of solitary nights, I could feel the sap rising dangerously.

I drove to Cambridge, mescaline in my pocket. I mentioned it right off. Janet was open to taking it with me. Her only question was about its quality.

Oh, the mescaline was good, I said. A guy at the farm had dropped some and an hour later, he was face down on the ground, humping Mother Earth. Back then, that constituted an endorsement. We popped the pills.

A psychedelic can take an hour to come on, so we went for a walk. It was a warm night, and the trees were newly heavy with leaves. For the ecstatic, Cambridge was a showcase: Anything green soon began to pulsate with life energy. Even the traffic lights were sending messages.

Somehow we found our way back to Janet's apartment. I didn't stumble to the record player and put an album on, as I usually would. I understood that on this night, we'd be the music. Slowly, as if we were swimming underwater, clothes dropped off. And then we sat, as languid as junkies, and just touched one another.

I can't reconstruct the physical part of the encounter, but I'm sure there was nothing special about any of it. The thrills were all internal. I'd never been more present, more responsive, more in sync with every move and emotion. Everything that happened seemed predestined and yet utterly surprising.

And the biggest surprise was the love I felt.

Not that Janet and I had a future. She'd go on to a man handsome enough for Hollywood, and marriages and kids; I would have a decade of broken romances before I married, for the first time, at thirty-nine. But the future wasn't an issue. There's nothing harder in life than being here now—giving the moment and your partner your complete attention. Well, I did.

Our orgasm was alchemy. One moment we were locked together, then we became one, and then . . . poof! No bodies, no names. We had disappeared.

I don't know where we went or how long we were gone, but the return was gentle. This was a new feeling, and it had unexpected power. We held each other and whispered, and there was a sweetness about those moments that was as thrilling as all that had gone before.

I've known a lot of gentleness since, and I've been the recipient of more female kindness and tenderness than I probably deserve. John Updike once described another writer as a man who saw woman as a giant lap. But I know I wasn't hiding from the world in the beds of my lovers; I was trying out a little tenderness, exposing myself, daring to risk.

Now I'm in my final marriage, and my wife is the beneficiary of lessons learned from the women who came before her. The weed has changed; now it comes from somewhere in Northern California. And the music's more international; we're as likely to play Nusrat Fateh Ali Khan as Led Zeppelin. But the essential transaction remains unchanged. Slowly, slowly, in bed with a woman, I am learning how to be human.

# IN BED WITH THE
# SUNDAY TIMES

CARY WONG

I CAME TO NEW YORK CITY to go to graduate school at Columbia University and to live out my dream of being a playwright—in the big time, not in just any rinky-dink city. I also came here to live out of the closet, something I couldn't do in Oakland, California, where I shared a home with my parents for the first twenty-one years of my life—even during undergraduate school at nearby UC Berkeley, when I commuted from home by bus or carpool.

I arrived in Manhattan in 1988, and for the next five years or so, my sexual liberation was limited to identity; it didn't involve any action, in keeping with my being a good, if lapsed, Catholic. I was focused on my career, and I ignored any distractions. Besides, the city was in the midst of the AIDS epidemic, and for that reason, sexual experimentation was not high on my agenda. But my focus eventually shifted.

I enjoyed many little career victories—a production at a prestigious theater festival, various readings around the country, and a playwriting fellowship—but the financial debt that usually accompanies an artistic calling was crushing me. I held a long succession of impressive, résumé-building, entertainment-related (and thus low-paying) jobs: in the press office of a major Off-Broadway theater, in the box office of *Blue Man Group*, at a company casting extras for major movies filming in New York, at a law firm handling A-list musicians, and even at a national gay magazine. But at this point in my life (my midthirties), I was sick of being in credit card hell, so I decided to work for at least a couple of years at a better-paying, lower-stress job.

The new job, however, left me too much time to think about the other deficits in my life, including, first and foremost, the absence of a meaningful relationship. Sure, I had many first dates, and even with Rudy Giuliani's crusade to clean up the city's image, New York still offered ample places for a young man to hook up. In fact, in the late '90s, these places, with their promises of easy (and always safe) sex and no strings attached, made long-term relationships seem unnecessary. But I have always been a romantic at heart, and by the turn of the new century, I felt I was missing out by being a lone wolf. Having a more mature perspective on my finances, I now wanted to be more mature about relationships.

Internet dating was becoming popular. It was more appealing than scanning (or running) those lonely hearts ads, so I latched on to dating Web sites for the next couple of years. Most men are not very creative with their descriptions of themselves and what they want in another man. Accordingly, just about everyone loves the outdoors but can be a homebody as well, enjoying reading the Sunday *New York Times* in bed with a partner, usually with a yellow Labrador at their feet. I'm not sure how this idyllic image entered our collective unconscious, but I bought into it and adopted it for my Internet dating profile.

My profile picture alone probably attracted a certain type of man, a rice queen (a hateful term, but there you go). I dated one once, for a couple of weeks, an older gentleman who had an apartment filled with Asian antiques and framed Chinese calligraphy. You know you're talking to a rice queen if, within ten minutes of meeting him, he asks, "Where are you from?" and is not satisfied if you answer, "Oakland." A guy is a hard-core Asian chaser if you say you're Chinese and he responds with an accent-perfect Mandarin phrase. And if that guy's wearing jade hanging from a gold chain around his neck, you might as well sign up for karate lessons and learn how to prune bonsai trees, for you are about to become General MacArthur's chicken. As I received responses to my online dating profile, it became obvious who was interested in the Asian aspect: obese or older men, or, if the stars were really shining on me, both.

Despite the many overtures from rice queens, the Internet dating experience was exciting at first, and fruitful: I had a fulfilling, eighteen-month relationship with a guy I met on one of the Web sites. (We're still good friends, but we just didn't see eye to eye as to what we really wanted from each other.) But after that early success, visiting the sites became demoralizing, as most e-mail exchanges seemed doomed before the first hello. Every time I checked my in-box, I felt closer to my fate as a bitter old maid. That's why what happened next seemed so odd. (This suddenly feels like a letter to *Honcho* magazine.)

On a humid summer night I was at a party in Chelsea where I didn't know anyone except the host, who was too busy to spend a lot of time talking to me. Most of the guests were paired up, and so I did the whole scanning-the-bookshelves bit, which quickly got old because the host had a minimalist decorating style. Then I noticed another single guy, in the kitchen, hanging near a cluster of Asian men. I wasn't sure if I wanted to handle the baggage of another rice queen, but this guy looked different from the others I had encountered. He was youngish—midthirties—height- and weight-appropriate (I don't need buff, but I do need appropriate), and he had the cutest smile. So when he walked away from the kitchen and settled down on the sofa in the living room, I decided to do what I rarely have done in situations like this: I became proactive. I made the initial eye contact, and when he didn't immediately look away as if I were Medusa about to turn him into stone, I sat next to him on the sofa and, nerves be damned, I started the awkward dance.

Linus (not his real name), thankfully, was a talkative guy. He worked for a nonprofit organization for kids and lived in New Jersey. He had been in a long-term relationship (with an Asian man—a red flag I chose to ignore) and was just beginning to go out again. His friend who invited him was running late, and he didn't know anyone else at the party. While I absorbed all this background information, I was feeling a connection between us that was electric. In fact, during the small talk—about ankles, of all things—our hands met halfway between us on the sofa, and neither of us made any motion to move them away.

Yes, I thought things were moving really fast, but what did I know about instant connection? Maybe this is how it felt. Finally, after almost twenty years in New York, had I actually found someone who was as into me as I was into him? Did the universe finally deem me worthy of being in a mature relationship? Or maybe it was just a physical reaction to each other, because after about an hour of talking, we sneaked out onto the host's roof and made out. I felt like a college kid, but it was exciting.

When we realized we had been gone from the party for too long, we stopped and made plans to have an official date in two days, and then exchanged phone numbers and e-mail addresses. I was practically giddy when I left the party. We e-mailed each other over the next couple of days, arranging to meet at a bar in Chelsea. In one of his e-mails Linus wrote that he felt as though he had a high school crush.

The date could not have been better. We held hands at the bar, asking silly questions about our lives—nothing too serious. We walked from the bar to the Christopher Street piers, where we looked out at Jersey and made out again. At dinner we talked about friends and family. As we said good-bye at the train station, we decided to take this one step further and meet at his place in New Jersey that weekend. Even before I got home, he texted me to let me know that he had fun. I had never sent a text message before with my cell phone, and it took a few tries before my phone let me know that it had delivered my reply, which was that I had fun, too.

Leading up to the weekend, I wrote an e-mail a day just to be goofy. Sometimes Linus e-mailed back, but more often then not, he didn't. That was okay, because he was outside the office most of the day, and this was before the advent of smart phones. But Friday came, and he still hadn't told me how to get to his place in Jersey. I e-mailed him and got no response. On Saturday morning I called him, but he didn't answer his phone. So I e-mailed him and asked if everything was okay, and that if something had come up, to just let me know. Nothing.

On Sunday, Linus finally e-mailed me and said that he thought things were moving too fast, that he had just broken up with his last boyfriend and didn't want to jump into another relationship so soon. We could slow down, I wrote; we could proceed at his pace. But after a bit of prodding, he confessed that he thought I was too intense, with all the e-mails and phone calls and texting (apparently, each of the texts I sent that first night went through). He ended his e-mail by saying that we should not contact each other again. As quickly as he had appeared in my life, he was gone.

It's now been three years since I met Linus. I sometimes rationalize that I'm living in a sort of *Truman Show* in which outside forces are keeping me single for their own amusement. Imagining this scenario actually soothes me, because I'm using my creative juices to rationalize what happened instead of wallowing in self-pity. The experience should have taught me that if there is someone as neurotic as Linus out there, there's also probably someone who isn't, and he and I are just waiting to meet. But instead of trying to find this man, I've decided to let him find me. This way there's less stress and fewer kicks to the self-esteem.

I've taken up playwriting again, but now less as a career option than for fun. And with my debt gone and my bank account in the black, I'm thinking about traveling the world or even buying a place of my own, things I have never before considered.

If I find true love, that will be great. But I need to be happy in my own life, because love is never an easy deal. I remember what a friend once told me about relationships in New York: "You can always do better." That's probably true, for better or worse. If you've just broken up with someone, another person will enter your life who is better than who you had. And if you're in a relationship, inevitably someone will come along who is better than who you have—or who your partner has. So this one-week ordeal with Linus convinced me to envision the next part of my life as a solo adventurer. While this may be a lonelier road to travel, the scenery is just as lovely, and I can stop at any point to enjoy the view.

I do lounge around in bed reading the Sunday *Times* (on my BlackBerry), but I also have the TV on, and it's tuned to a new program in which New York City real estate brokers show apartments and houses that are available. These days, this is what turns me on.

# TALKING SHOP

REGIE O'HARE GIBSON

I OCCASIONALLY PARTICIPATE in something called the Man Panel, a monthly gathering at a local bar where single women drink wine and pepper a lineup of men of various backgrounds with questions about dating and relationships. Yes, dangerous. I know.

The typical questions are hurled at us: *What do you find attractive in a woman? What determines if you approach a woman? How important is good sex in a relationship?*

To which most of us men give stock answers: *If she's hot! If she's really hot! Very!*

However, every now and then a finely lipsticked mouth will shoot a zinger at us with so much heat on it we just want to duck and get out of the way. Here's one of them: *What childhood memories and experiences affected you as a man and, subsequently, your relationship with women?*

Owww! I've been hit!

I desperately tried not to let this question bother me, but it did. The angel that said, "Go ahead. Grappling with the question will be good for you and make you a better man," was getting his ass kicked by the id that said, "To hell with that! Just be hip and urbane. Let some other poor fool field this one." But because I am a poet, my penchant for public masochism won out over my common sense. I knew I had to confront the question. I slowly lifted my hand and said, "I'll try it." The guys to my right and left were relieved. I think I heard one of them say Whew!

Here's the answer I gave, recounted and expanded.

Sometimes I travel my self. That is to say, I project myself back to boyhood and dig the cultural, social, and religious water in which I once waded. Right now I'm in 1977. Just roll with me on this one.

I am nine. It's a typical Chicago summer, hot and urban, with the smell of barbecue and hot sauce spanking the air as though it were a disobedient three-year-old. My younger brother, Ron, and I are in Mother's beauty shop, Gibson's House of Styles. Today is Saturday, the day she sculpts the heathen heads of women into shapes God will accept in church tomorrow morning. Today my mother is a conjure woman, hard at work on her customers' illusions. Her eye of newt and toe of frog? Sulfur 8 and lanolin shampoo. Her wool of bat and tongue of dog? Dark and Lovely and #8 black rinse. We watch as hair, once as unreasonable as a slumlord on the eighth of the month, surrenders to the merciless teeth of the black straightening comb—instrument of torture, agent of beauty.

I can remember every one of these women's names: Miss Dorthee, Miss Moshell, Miss Dareese . . . they are every sepia shade imaginable. Some are as wide as a Sunday-morning church hat. Some are as skinny as they swear they will make their men's wallets come Monday.

*You damn right, I'm my own woman! I don't need no man to take care of me.*

*I know what you mean, girl! I'd do alright by myself too, and believe me my man better know it! And my man know that he better be payin' for what's on this head if he wants what's in these pants . . .*

Their collective laughter is fever-pitched in the blow-dried air. Livening their mouths are momentary glints of gold or silver teeth, giving away the Mississippi they came from.

*If a man don't wanna put clothes on your back then you don't let him put you on yours!*

*Girl, you sho' is right about that! Some say it's what's up front that counts, but if a man ain't got dollars then bein' with him just don't make no sense.*

I look up at my mother's hands. They are busy hexing a head of hair. I look at myself, look over at my brother. He is staring at the television, lost in Saturday morning animation. But I am living the cartoon. *Is this what women really think, or are they just saying these things to get a laugh? Is this the way it really is between men and women? Did any of the men know this? Oh no, is my mother like them?*

So how have these childhood memories and experiences affected me as a man and, subsequently, my relationship with women?

I can understand if you've drawn the conclusion that I don't have a very high opinion of the women in the beauty shop. But that's untrue. These women always treated me well. They were both formidable and kind. They handled their homes and children well, and despite their weekly reaming-of-the-man ritual, most of the women took care of the men in their lives in a loving, albeit heavy-handed, fashion. Still, I've been distrustful of women, fearing that one day a woman might give kisses on the face and on another day a knife in the back, and that women are materialistic and selfish and are only out for what they can get.

However, my closest friends have been women. Perhaps my confusion over what I call my "beauty-shop moments" has caused me to seek out genuine friendships with women. When I have related some of my fears to my women friends, more than a handful have said that they have sometimes felt the need to reduce a relationship to things monetary to compensate for a relationship's lack of intimacy, communication, and simple courtesy.

So I have learned to conduct periodic "relationship check-ins" with the women in my life—whether the relationship is familial, romantic, or platonic. I don't care what a man says; if he is honest, he will admit that a large part of his self-image hinges upon how he is perceived by the women around him.

And I have learned a few things about becoming a better husband, father, and man. I have learned the importance of preparing my home to receive a woman; this shows respect for her and for myself. I have learned to ask questions at least as much as I make statements, to be careful about raising my voice in anger—far too many women have experienced yelling as a prelude to violence—and to show strength and sensitivity. That is, to be respectful of women but not a fool for them. Yes, this might be fortune-cookie stuff, but it's still good advice.

Confronting the question honestly has become part of a psychological journey that has been delightful and disturbing, nostalgic and nasty—but also necessary in my ongoing quest to understand this ever-shifting thing called manhood.

# SILENCE

JOE D'ARRIGO

WHEN IT WAS CLEAR that the end was near, and the doctors said they would make Pat as comfortable as possible in the hospital, she said, "I'll go home, thank you." It was Thanksgiving; Christmas was coming, and she wanted to spend it at home, with her family.

I turned the playroom into a hospital room, a hospital bed replaced the couch in the family room, the refrigerator was stocked with feeding supplements, medical supplies were delivered, and hospice was contacted. We would spend these last few weeks together in the house that we had shared for the last twenty years, the place where our five children had grown up.

Pat was crying when the ambulance pulled into our driveway. She knew that she was returning to her home for the last time. The doctors said it would be a matter of weeks, that most likely Pat would not make it to Christmas.

All the children were home. Kerri and Beth had graduated from college and were living nearby. Jen was home from college on trimester break, Kate was finishing treatment—successfully—for her own bout with cancer, and Matt was taking a year off from school. We sat with Pat twenty-four hours a day. She was never to be alone at night. An easy chair was moved to the side of the bed so someone would always be there.

We celebrated Christmas Day as we had for each of the last twenty years. A fire roared in the fireplace as we sat around the living room—Pat with her portable stanchion with the morphine drip and feeding bags and tubes—and exchanged presents, and then we had breakfast. It was a glorious and bittersweet day.

That night, when the children were out or asleep, Pat decided it was time to stop hanging on. She had shared this last Christmas with her family, and now she was ready. She told me she wanted the feeding tube removed. The doctors assured us that it would be a matter of days.

· · · ·

Before Pat became sick, we had come to a comfortable stage of our lives. Pat was in a career she loved, working as a nurse in a hospital. My business was doing well. The kids were in college or had graduated; we were down to three tuitions from six—it was as though we had hit the lottery. We had money, and we had time. In November, on a whim, we went to Bermuda for a long weekend. Not bad for two kids from Queens.

We had plans. The kids would be getting married, so we decided to learn how to waltz. We took our first lesson in January, at an Arthur Murray studio. We were not very graceful, but we had some laughs. We had a pizza after that first lesson, in a restaurant that had to be the only one in the world with an indoor boccie court. The next night, Pat was in the hospital.

She had not been feeling well for a couple of months. On our trip to Bermuda she felt a little off but could not put a finger on what was wrong. She went to a doctor, a good family friend, for a checkup. I accompanied her, thinking we would have lunch afterward.

The doctor sent Pat to the hospital that afternoon for some tests. He knew something was wrong but wasn't sure what it was. She was admitted, thinking she would be home in a few days. Those days turned into a week as doctors searched for a diagnosis, conducting every test imaginable: MRIs, X-rays, scopes, blood tests on a daily basis. Pat's hospital room became our home, and the windowsill became her bookshelf. She passed the time studying Scripture (Pat had earned a master's degree in theology from Harvard Divinity School), reading Shakespeare, or knitting, as our frustration grew.

Each day I would get up at 5:00 a.m., go for a run, and then go to the hospital, arriving at about 6:15. I would go to the cafeteria, get a coffee and the newspaper, and then go to Pat's room to be there when she woke up. We would talk, read the paper, and then wait for the morning rounds to find out what the day's plan was. But there never seemed to be a plan.

Pat had been in the hospital for five weeks when she was diagnosed with a rare tropical disease. It affected a valve between the stomach and the intestines, not allowing the free flow of liquids. Doctors tried various treatments and medications but to no effect. Because Pat was a nurse, none of the medical jargon was lost on her. Another two weeks passed before my frustration reached the breaking point. On the Friday before Presidents' Day weekend, after I had engaged in a heated exchange with the surgical chief, the hospital agreed to allow exploratory surgery.

The operation was Saturday, and I waited outside the operating room, pacing for hours in a basement-level corridor. The corridor, painted green, had a Coke machine and a pay phone at the far end, and the only light came from tiny windows well above eye level. When the surgeon emerged, he was pale and looking at the floor as he approached me. Pat had stomach cancer, he said. She was loaded. He did the best he could to remove all he could see, but it didn't look good. Most likely she had only a couple of weeks, a couple of months at the most. When he turned and left, I looked at the pay phone. Who could I call? I needed to scream. I needed to say the words, that Pat had cancer. I needed to be heard. I needed to be held. I didn't know what I needed.

I called my friend Don, and as I said the words, the dam broke and the tears rolled down my face. Then I called my friend Bill. I couldn't think. I just needed to talk.

Over the next couple of days we learned that the form of stomach cancer Pat had was especially deadly; people with it had only a 5 percent survival rate. The fight was on.

Pat was offered a chance to go to New York City for an experimental treatment, and she accepted it with little hesitation. As soon as she was able to get on a plane we were off to New York with copies of her MRI and medical records. Before she could begin the treatments, Pat had to undergo another operation, to make sure all the cancer was removed and to insert a shunt for the chemicals she would be treated with. It was St. Patrick's Day. Pat had marched in New York's parade each year she was in nursing school at St. Vincent's, wearing the flowing cape and the big, pointy hat that distinguished the St. Vincent's nurses.

Pat got out of bed the day after the operation. She was determined to beat this. She dragged the various stanchions, with IVs flowing, into the bathroom to wash her face. She just wanted to move to prove she could. The plan was for her to regain her strength, go back home when she could travel, rest, and then return to New York for chemo treatment.

Two days after the operation I went home and bought a sailboat, a thirty-footer that I named *Expectations*. Pat and I had talked of buying a sailboat when the kids were out of college. I returned to New York with a picture of the boat and I pinned it to the hospital-room wall. The treatment would be over by mid-June, and we would sail out of Newport, Rhode Island, that summer. This would work. It had to work. While Pat recovered, I decided, I would continue to manage the process, to stay busy, to plan for all contingencies. Being in control seemed like the objective, to stay in constant motion, to only occasionally sneak a glimpse of the void.

We spent the next few months traveling back and forth to New York for treatment. Each trip sapped more strength from Pat. She was becoming frail before my eyes. But after the treatments were finished, Pat's strength slowly returned. She spent her days reading, studying, taking care of her house, attending to her garden. She was gaining weight.

She began taking longer walks. Sweatpants, purple socks, sneakers, and she was off. Within a couple of months she was running, to the beach, up the glades and back.

We did go sailing on *Expectations* a few times. Pat was still weak, and sometimes she would wrap herself in a blanket and sit belowdecks to keep warm. I would ask her if she wanted to go back. "No," she would say. A cup of soup and a blanket and she would be fine. We had one overnight on the boat. We left Newport Harbor in the early evening with a bottle of red wine and a bag of chips and the sails filled. We headed up Narragansett Bay, sailed under the bridge, came about, and navigated into Potter Cove. The sun was setting as we sat on deck, each of us with a glass of wine. The evening chill forced us below, and there we snuggled and spent the night rocking gently to the ripples of the water and listening to the sounds of the bay.

Pat continued to grow stronger every day. I returned to work on a full-time basis, cautiously optimistic that we had made it. She was running a couple of miles a few times a week and back to studying, this time for a PhD in Gaelic history.

In October, Pat started to feel as though something was wrong. She had an MRI, but it showed no signs of cancers. Though the doctors said she was in remission, Pat's body was telling her something different.

The third week in November she went back in the hospital. Her pain was overwhelming. The surgeon told us that he would not operate on Pat. She was loaded with cancer, he said, and he didn't feel he should operate, even to relieve her pain. Pat's pain was excruciating, and nothing was being done.

We moved Pat to another hospital in the middle of the night. Shortly after we arrived, a surgical team assessed her condition and made arrangements to operate within an hour. The surgeon said he would speak with me as soon as the operation was over.

It was three o'clock in the morning when he opened the door. The cancer was back and had spread throughout her abdomen, he said. It would be a matter of weeks, if that long. It was time to end the fight.

· · · ·

In the days following that last Christmas, we didn't talk about the past. We talked about the future. We spoke of the sorrow, of missing our children's weddings and the births of their children, our grandchildren. We talked about her funeral, the eulogy I would give, the music, her burial. Pat was not controlling, but she did have specific requests. She wanted her service to be a simple one.

She spoke of meeting God. She had some questions for him. She wanted to know why there were no women priests, whether that was His idea.

The doctors said she had only days, but those became a week, and then a second week. With morphine as her only sustenance, her body withered away. But Pat remained alert, reading *The Catholic Moment* every day and underlining passages as if there was going to be a quiz when she finished. She would struggle to get out of bed just to walk around the kitchen island.

I changed her dressings, gave her massages, and rubbed peppermint cream on her feet. I needed help from the hospice nurse those last few days because I just couldn't change the dressings anymore without crying. Pat weighed only sixty pounds then.

Early one morning she leaned over to me, and with tears in her eyes she said, "I love you so very much." We kissed. She wanted to apologize for whatever she thought she might have done wrong in the thirty-five years we spent together. There was nothing to apologize for.

We sat in silence for a long time, and then she wanted to talk about my future, telling me that I should date, get remarried, go on with life. I didn't want to talk about those things.

A week later, one brilliantly sunny January afternoon, I was sitting beside Pat, not really paying attention, looking up at a frozen, crystal blue sky, when she took her last breath. Her breathing had always been quiet, but at that instant there was silence, and I knew she was gone. I had thought I would be prepared for this, that I was in control, that I would be OK. But that final moment is as vivid today as it was almost seventeen years ago. That silence was the loudest sound I have ever heard.

I held Pat's hand for a while before finally getting up and kissing her warm face.

# STRUCTURAL FAILURE

**AMIN AHMAD**

I ALWAYS LET PETER go through the door first. You never know who's on the other side. It could be a man with a gun. Peter bangs on the door and shouts, "Anybody home? We got to inspect your apartment! It's just me, the janitor, and an architect!" Silence follows.

Peter, a short and wiry man with close-cropped gray hair, unlocks the door and pokes his head into the room. "Nobody home," he says, with a grin. "All safe. We can go in."

I start breathing again. It was Peter who told me how he once had entered a dark apartment and found a revolver aimed at his head. He has plenty of stories; he's been a janitor in these Boston projects for twenty-two years.

The temperature inside the apartment is stifling. Peter turns on the lights and we watch the roaches scuttle for cover. I take out my clipboard and we start the inspection: Sagging floors indicate structural failure; green stains on the walls are mold; buckled tiles hide water leaks.

The worst part of the inspections involves the stained toilet bowls. You sit on them and rock from side to side. In deference to my status as an architect, Peter checks the toilets. "This one's loose," he says.

"Hey, you see the cricket match, man?" Peter asks.

He and I are cricket fans. He's Trinidadian. I'm Indian. We both are immigrants, both brown men. Brown men have to do the worst work. It's what we have in common. We understand this.

It's late afternoon now, and the winter light is fading. The apartment we're inspecting is furnished with bare mattresses, and crimson-stained sanitary pads litter the floor. On the wall are rows of framed photographs of children. The glass in each frame has been shattered, and the cracks cover the kids' smiles. In this dim, fractured space, I think about my wife, and how the fights have worsened. Last night she tried to kill herself by emptying a bottle of sedatives into her mouth. I had to stick my fingers into her mouth and pry out the pills. Then we fought, with whispered threats, tortured breathing, the thud of her fists on my chest. I just prayed that our son would not wake up.

"Ooof, man, I'm tired," Peter says. "Let's get us some coffee. We got 185 apartments to do. Gotta pace ourselves."

I want to tell Peter that I'm tired too, tired of this shit. But Peter is a Jehovah's Witness, and cursing upsets him. So I just nod instead.

Outside, it's almost dark now, and freezing. I walk bareheaded beside Peter toward the coffee shop.

"Peter. Can I ask you something? You've been married a long time, right?"

Peter, his face half hidden beneath a thick knit cap, nods.

"Yup, thirty-seven years. You want to know the secret? Young guys always want to know the secret."

He chuckles and looks up at me.

"The secret is you got to talk. Talk about everything. And sometimes, to get the right woman, you just got to be lucky. Luck, that's all there is to it. Your wife, she Indian?"

"Yes, we met in India. She doesn't like it here."

"Yeah, it's tough here. This cold—all this." Peter spreads his arms, motioning to include the cold, gray evening, the garbage piles on the sidewalk, the junkies nodding on the stoops. "She'll get used to it, man. Just be kind, be gentle."

. . . .

The coffee shop is warm and filled with the rich smell of burnt coffee. Ray and Chuck have a table by the window and wave us over. They're both janitors, both older men from the Deep South. Chuck is still handsome and wears his blue overalls with fighter-pilot élan. Ray has a long, sunken face and a raggedy goatee.

"So," asks Peter, straddling a chair that he has turned backward, "what you two been doing today, slacking off, now that I ain't there to bust your lazy asses?"

Ray and Chuck grin and blow steam off their coffees.

"Well, there was that one busted screen we repaired," Chuck says.

Ray raises two fingers in a V.

"Make that two busted screens," Chuck says with a smile.

I drink my coffee and listen to them talk about broken windows, rat problems, and illegal washing machines. I've been having coffee with these men for weeks now. I've heard Ray and Chuck's stories about traveling from Alabama to Boston in the early '60s, desperate for work, and how janitor jobs were the only ones available for a black man. They dream about someday returning home. They want to spend their old age dozing and fishing. The present for all of us is just something to be endured until we can get back to our real lives. Ray turns to me and in a gravelly voice says, "My man, I gotta talk to you. These boilers you people is installing. They're no good."

"They're high-efficiency," I say. "Good for the environment."

"Yeah, man, but how you expect me to get up a head of steam with a twenty-pound boiler? I need me a fi'ty-pound boiler—at least." Peter and Chuck smile into their coffees. Boilers are Ray's life. We call his lament the Boiler Blues.

"I have to pick up my son. See you guys tomorrow," I say, gulping down my coffee. I hear a murmur of farewell as I head out the door to run for the bus.

At the day care center I stop in the doorway of my son's class and search the room for his round, dark head. He is in a corner, building a tower of blocks, concentrating deeply. My son has his mother's eyes, but his round cheeks come directly from my brother, and the way he frowns reminds me of my mother. I walk over to him, pick him up, bury my nose in his hair, and smell the world.

. . . .

It is getting very cold. I spend every workday in the South End with Peter, surveying apartments. We have become like an old married couple, communicating in gestures, finishing each other's sentences.

We go into the top-floor apartment of a brownstone that is settling. Jagged cracks appear in the foundation, and the stairs lean drunkenly. This whole area of the South End is landfill, and the houses have been built on centuries of garbage. "This baby's funky," Peter says. "It's a six, for sure."

"Yup," I say, knowing he means a total gut: new ceilings, new floors, new Sheetrock on the walls. But because of the slant of the floors, I'm also thinking there's structural failure. While I try to imagine how we're going to fix this building, Peter stands stock-still in the middle of the room. His nose is quivering like a hunting dog's.

"Something's wrong," he says, gesturing to the kitchen stove. All the knobs are missing.

"What? We're going to need a new stove?"

"Shhh, listen."

The room is quiet except for the gurgle of heating pipes and the scratch-scratch of pigeons on the windowsill. Then I hear it: a faint, high-pitched keening sound.

Peter flings open the door of the living room closet. Cowering inside are two little boys. The older one—he's maybe five—is clamping his hand over the younger one's mouth, trying to silence his crying. They are both filthy, with snotty, crusted noses.

Peter kneels in front of them.

"It's okay. It's okay. We're not going to hurt you. Where's your mommy, at work?"

The older boy glares up, but the baby—he's no older than three, no older than my son—nods, still crying. Peter gently takes the little boy into his arms, fishes out a handkerchief, and wipes his face.

"Call social services," Peter says. He reels off a number, and I dial it on my cell phone. A woman tells me someone will be there in half an hour.

We sit down on a battered couch with the kids, the baby in my lap, the five-year-old in Peter's. Both the children fall asleep, exhausted from crying. It feels so familiar to have a warm child in my arms, sleeping peacefully.

I remember the first morning in the hospital after my son was born. Cradling him, I looked out at the city and whispered, "Baby, I'm your father, and I will always take care of you."

And I have. I pick him up from day care every day, take him home and bathe him, dance with him in my arms until he falls asleep. When my wife returns from work she scoops him up and croons, "Oh, my baby, my poor baby. Never mind, your mother is home." Then she takes him into another room.

Later at night my wife and I argue about my low-paying job, about the money we do not have to buy a house. Ignoring our finances, my wife plans a trip to India. She wants to get off the plane like a movie star, with suitcases full of presents for her relatives. She retreats into her three-hour-long Hindi movies and when I touch her, she snarls at me. I have become the symbol of her unhappiness.

In the apartment, the baby's face is pushed into my chest, soaking it with drool. When the social services woman arrives, the baby wakes with a start and looks up at me. His eyes are big; he's afraid. I feel as though I'm handing over my own son.

The woman departs, the children crying all the way down the stairs. Peter's face is ashen.

"I knew it, from the stove," he says softly. "When they leave the kids alone they take the knobs off."

I'm still sitting on the couch, looking at the wet spot on my shirt where the baby's head had just been. "What is happening to this world?" Peter continues. "These little babies left alone. And you can't blame the woman. Her husband's gone, left her alone. She's got to get a job, feed those hungry mouths.

I close my eyes tight. My breath comes in ragged gasps.

"Hey, you okay, man?" Peter walks over and touches my shoulder. "These things happen. You gotta let it go."

When I open my eyes, they are filled with tears.

"Let's go get us some hot coffee," Peter says. "That's what we need."

. . . .

We take our usual seats at the coffee shop, by the plate glass window. My hands are shaking so badly that I scald myself.

"What's going on, man?" Peter looks at me over the rim of his coffee cup.

"Peter, it's bad. We're fighting all the time. She says she'll kill herself."

"Your wife? She serious?"

"I don't know. It's killing me."

"You talk to her? You try, whatchamacallit, counseling?"

I nod dumbly. We tried a therapist, an Indian woman who told us smugly that Indians don't get divorced, that we would just have to learn to live with each other.

"My wife's like a kid. I can't trust her alone with my son."

"Slow down, man. Drink your coffee. Breathe."

The coffee is burnt and hot. Its sourness coils my stomach.

"I want to leave my marriage. I can't handle it anymore."

I've never said these words before. I would never dare say this to my family or to my Indian friends. Nobody in our family has ever divorced. *Indians don't get divorced.* Divorce is failure. Divorce is the destruction of the home. Divorce is to become like the Americans who are barbarians and abandon their families.

Peter's eyes widen.

"You sure you want to leave your wife?"

"I know it's completely wrong. I know it's a horrible thing to do and . . ."

"Listen to me."

I look up at Peter, at his calm eyes. He speaks slowly, carefully choosing his words.

"Listen. You're a good man. I know that. You love your son. But you got to look after yourself first. Understand? If you're no good, there's nothing you can do for him. You hear me?"

I nod again. I have heard him. They're the first words I've heard in a long time.

"I'll finish the other two apartments," Peter says. "You finish your coffee. Then take a walk. Clear your head, man. No arguments."

I watch Peter leave, a small man in his olive drab janitor's uniform, hunched against the cold.

. . . .

It is deep winter. When I leave work now, I don't go home. My boss, hearing that I had no place to live, found me a studio apartment in the projects. It's on the ground floor and it has bars on the windows. All day and night I hear sirens, screams, muttering. I keep the shades tightly pulled; all that separates me from the street is a few millimeters of vinyl.

I call in sick and sleep all day. In the evening I take the bus across town to pick up my son at day care. We go to a coffee shop. To entertain him, I make men out of coffee stirrers and straws. My son gurgles when he laughs. Then his mother comes and takes him away. He is confused and looks back at me over her shoulder.

I call in sick the next three days, and on the fourth I wake up, put on my hard hat and go to work, to the town house where Peter and I had found the two little boys. The structural engineer is coming today to evaluate the building.

The inside of the house is unrecognizable. The walls and ceilings have been stripped of their Sheetrock cladding. What were once rooms are now only wooden cages. The place smells of freshly cut wood, power tools, and workmen's sweat.

The structural engineer and I walk through all four floors, noting the slant of the stairway and the slope of the beams.

"Wood never fails catastrophically, like steel," he tells me, pointing to places where the beams are sagging. "It just sags for years before breaking. It gives you plenty of warning."

Peter clambers up the stairs, wearing a yellow hard hat that is too large for him.

"Hey, stranger. Haven't seen you this week. How ya doin'?"

"Fine, fine," I say, but Peter sees the dark circles under my eyes.

"Ray and Chuck and them was asking about you. Come by the coffee shop later, okay?"

I nod and carry on working with the engineer. As soon as I can, I hurry to the coffee shop. It is just past three, but the afternoon is already sliding into night.

The coffee shop is empty except for Peter, who is sitting in a corner. A few minutes later Ray and Chuck amble in. They insist on buying me a Boston cream doughnut. Chuck looks as handsome as ever, with immaculately barbered hair, but the winter has been tough on Ray. He's had pneumonia, and he still coughs hollowly.

"So," says Chuck, looking at me. "How's your new place?"

"It's OK," I say. "There are mice and stuff. But it's temporary, you know."

"Mice. Shit. Keep all your food inside the fridge. Coffee, sugar, everything. Then they won't bother you. You got a date yet?"

I must look confused, because Chuck continues. "I mean a court date. Peter told us."

"Umm, no, we're just separated. We have to reach a settlement first. She doesn't want to let me see my son as much as I want."

Ray leans in, coughing. His cheeks are gaunt and covered with a day-old beard.

"That shit is tough. Been through it myself. Married this gal down South. She was no good. Had to cut her loose. But it tore me up. Still tears me up."

"Yeah," Chuck adds. "How's your son?"

"He's okay," I say. "Hard to tell."

"Kids are tough, man. They survive. Important thing is, you keep seeing him."

There is an awkward silence. Then Ray clears his throat.

"Those boilers, man. Those new boilers you put in. They're killing me. Three buildings down already."

Peter and Chuck nudge each other and start laughing.

"Ray, you like a broken gramophone record, man," Peter says. "Give the boy a break."

"Gramophone? Shit. There're no gramophones anymore. All CDs these days. You all still got gramophones in Trinidad?"

Ray laughs so hard at his own joke that he coughs and has to thump his chest to stop.

It is almost four now. Time to pick up my son from day care. As I've done so many times before, I take my leave of the three men. I shake their hands, and as I walk out the door, Peter waves farewell.

I wait for the bus at the corner. Across the road is the leaning town house. It is barely visible in the twilight, but I can see a red X above the front door, a warning that the building is structurally unsound. The building will never be plumb and square, but we're going to lift up the framing with hydraulic jacks, reinforce the beams, and rebuild most of the cracked facade. In a year's time, the building will be transformed, reclaimed from decay.

The bus arrives, and as we pull away from the curb, I try to imagine what my life will be like in another year. A knot forms in my stomach. Then I remind myself that a year from now, my three friends will still be here, sitting in the coffee shop. As the bus gathers speed and roars off into the darkness, I close my eyes and hear Peter, Ray, and Chuck telling stories. I hear their slow voices, their deliberate pauses, their full-bellied laughter.

On any dark day, I'll be able to walk into the coffee-scented warmth and they will welcome me without a word, without questions. I can pull up a chair, sit among them, and slowly sip my burnt coffee. In this cold, foreign city filled with pain, I know there is one place that will take me in.

# THE NOT-SO-DOLCE VITA

### MARK ST. AMANT

IN SEPTEMBER OF 2001, three months after we married, Celia and I up and moved to Italy. Six months later we returned to the States, almost broke and, somehow, still married.

"Up and moved" implies that this was a scheme we had hatched while crashed on the couch in our underwear, watching *Cops* and eating pepperoni Hot Pockets. Or that the World Trade Center attacks had jolted us into a radical, life's-too-short course of action. But actually, we had been planning the move ever since making a drunken New Year's Eve resolution (is there any other kind?) nearly ten months prior. That night, we promised each other that after we were married we would begin our new life by doing something . . . different. We had no idea what "different" meant, but we did know this: She was twenty-nine, I was thirty-three, and we both were more than ready for the emotional commitment of marriage but still too young for any kind of physical permanence. The notion of getting married, immediately moving to the burbs, having 2.5 kids, getting a golden retriever and a rider mower and a sump pump, and slogging away at our advertising jobs (I was a copywriter, she a producer) for the next thirty years reminded us of a certain scene from Pink Floyd's *The Wall*: We didn't want to be two more faceless drones shuffling on life's conveyor belt toward the meat grinder.

That New Year's Eve, in 2000, while gorging ourselves on piles of salted, cured meats with some friends at an Italian joint in Boston's North End, we remembered we each had a dream that just happened to fit the other's like a jigsaw piece: She had always wanted to live abroad and learn a foreign language; I had always wanted to feed my inner Hemingway, live in an exotic, faraway land, and have time to write something more creatively fulfilling than McDonald's commercials. Not that I believed my writing would be the literary equivalent of the polio vaccine, but I at least hoped to contribute something more beneficial to society than helping people waddle toward morbid obesity.

Maybe it was because we were loopy on a couple of gallons of Chianti, had recently been swept up in *Sopranos* mania, or were feeling cocky because New Year's resolutions were, by nature, hypothetical, but by the time we were back home watching the immortal Dick Clark host the Times Square ball drop, we had boldly agreed: Yes, damn it, we would get married that June, quit our jobs, and move to Italy.

• • • •

We arrived in Milan in the middle of the night, and despite our disorientation and kindergarten-level Italian ("Where I was saying, bread cheese man, we will make travel on big trains?"), soon managed to reach Florence, our new home. We found a small apartment two blocks from the majestic Duomo, a couple of doors down from the former home of Dante Alighieri.

Our mornings began with caffe lattes, fruit, and freshly baked bread, after which Celia would walk through the idyllic Piazza della

Repubblica to go to her language classes. I would find a nearby café, settle in, and enjoy a few consecutive hours of blissfully uninterrupted writing. After a few weeks, she was speaking Italian with a touch more confidence, and I was getting my book, about our move to Italy, into shape. (A publisher in San Francisco called Travelers' Tales eventually would accept one of the chapters for its annual travel humor anthology, and pay me $100 for it.) Our respective lifelong dreams were slowly coming together. But our months-long marriage was quickly falling apart.

Newlywed life abroad was often a fiendish torture that our neighbor Dante would have considered too harsh for his nine circles of Hell. We fought about everything. Tiny decisions became multistage debates. Meals became interminable staring contests. *What'd you do today, honey? Oh, right, I was with you for nine of the past eleven hours. We have nothing to say, and now—no offense, dear—I want to smash your goddamn face with this leg of prosciutto.*

Say what you will about the nine-to-five world that we had left behind, but it does give you some much-needed structure to your days, something we had no idea we would so dearly miss. "I sometimes picked fights with you at meals just so we'd have something to talk about," Celia admitted later, as if this weren't borderline sociopathic behavior.

No one tells you how difficult the first year of marriage is under normal circumstances, let alone when you (a) are suddenly living in a foreign country, (b) don't know another living soul, (c) still don't speak the language very well, (d) reside in a 500-square-foot studio apartment, and (e) don't know how long your meager savings will last. We had unwittingly enlisted in marriage boot camp, and we were washing out. My parents had been happily married for forty years, and here I was struggling to get through four months.

Changes of scenery didn't help. From Florence, we traveled to some of the most stunning places on Earth: Chianti, Lucca, Rome, the Amalfi Coast, Cinque Terre, Lake Como, Austria, Switzerland, Bavaria, Monaco, the south of France, Spain. But more often than not, we arrived at these places long after dark—and after having driven a car or ridden a train for hours—foolishly assuming that we would just wing it and find a cheap hotel. This would inevitably lead to more arguing about how much to spend, what was the best way to go, how to read a map—you name it, we fought about it. But who was she to second-guess me? She had lived in Boston for ten years and still got lost on our block. "Oh, definitely, you have a *much* stronger sense of direction than I do," she admitted once, while we were hopelessly lost in the chaos of Barcelona's La Rambla (which is, of course, Spanish for "street teeming with imbeciles who can't find the Gaudí Museum"). Her patronizingly cheerful tone nearly brought me to tears of full-blown rage. "But I have a stronger will than you," she continued. "And let's be honest, I'm right more often than you are. So it's unfortunately kind of a stalemate."

I'm not a violent person, but there was this other time, in Innsbruck, when we misplaced our rental car, because, in daylight, neither of us could remember how to find the garage where we had parked the previous night. (I honestly believe foreign municipal employees rearrange their city streets while we tourists sleep, just to screw with our heads.) While Celia blamed me for our missing Fiat Punto, I imagined hoisting our massive rolling suitcase over my head and crushing her with it. Her feet would stick out from underneath, like the Wicked Witch of the East's, and tiny, lollipop-wielding Austrians would emerge from manholes and nearby flora and gleefully raise their helium-filled voices to the skies, thanking me for ridding their kingdom of such evil. Then we would all eat some *schweinsbraten*.

• • • •

Celia and I finally hit rock bottom in January 2002, back in Florence. After a particularly heated argument—probably about money, or maybe I ate her last almond *cantuccini*, who knows—I grabbed my wallet, my passport, and my laptop and stormed out of the apartment to "get some air." But truth be told, I was leaving her. I was going to take a cab to the airport and buy a one-way ticket back to Boston, cost be damned. What would happen to her? How would she get home? Would she be worried when I didn't come back? I didn't care. I was done.

But in my wild-eyed, foam-mouthed walkabout (it was kind of a blur, but I imagine my fellow pedestrians gave me a wide berth, pulling their children closer to them as I stormed by), I had not headed toward the Duomo, where the closest cabstand was. Instead I had gone in the opposite direction, to the Ponte Vecchio, one of our favorite spots in the city.

It's one of man's most timeless creations, so beautiful that it was the only Florentine bridge that Hitler, the sentimental fool, declined to destroy during Germany's 1944 retreat from Allied troops. Amid a constantly flowing tide of jewelry-hunting tourists, frenetic locals, and North African street vendors peddling fake Gucci, Fendi, and Prada purses, I stood and just stared down the river. As the sun set with a purple-red flourish, I looked across the south bank and up to Piazza Michelangelo, where Celia and I had hiked so many times to enjoy the most spectacular view of our adopted hometown.

The piazza was high upon a hill and maybe a full mile away, but I still imagined Michelangelo's David, the epitome of the perfect man (even in bronze replica), fixating on me with his slightly furrowed brow and soulful yet challenging eyes. "Don't look at me like that," I muttered. I remained on the bridge for an hour, maybe more, long enough for me to forget what Celia and I had been fighting about, not just earlier that evening, but for the past five months.

Instead, I remembered celebrating her thirtieth birthday on Capri, how we rode a creaky rental moped to the famous Blue Grotto. She had her arms wrapped tightly around my torso, and we shrieked and laughed, and our goofy, *Star Wars* imperial stormtrooper–sized helmets occasionally clacked against one another as we took precarious corners and snaked up and down the narrow streets to the remote, northwestern shore of the island. And when we learned that the grotto was closed for the season, a discovery that might have reduced us to bickering cannibals—*Um, no, you were supposed to check the Frommer's book!*—we instead had a moment of unity. Standing there above the Mediterranean, we basked in the unseasonably warm November sun and in the eerie realization that not another soul on Earth knew our whereabouts, and should we hold hands, jump off the rocky cliffs into the sea, and just start swimming, our next stop (tide and sharks permitting) would be Tunisia. I felt a surge of romantic, adventurous liberation knowing that we were totally alone yet completely together in a place, and in a moment, in which we never could have imagined ourselves just a few months before.

This memory triggered an avalanche of other discreetly sublime moments I'd forgotten: attending English-language movies at the majestic Odeon theater, sitting high in the balcony under the ornate, domed ceiling and sharing popcorn as if it were our first date, so happy to be hearing our native tongue that we didn't care what was playing (hence our seeing *Bridget Jones's Diary* twice); strolling through the Uffizi Gallery and quietly joking that they could really use a few more *Madonna and Child* paintings. I remembered how we had faced outwardly mundane yet wholly intimidating everyday tasks: ordering meat or cheese at a crowded *salumeria*; realizing we had to weigh our fruits and vegetables and sticker them ourselves before getting in the supermarket checkout line; calculating how many lire we needed for your basic white load at the Laundromat; cracking the veritable da Vinci codes of the Florentine bus system or the post office hours of operation. When completed, these chores might elicit a satisfied high five or sometimes even a joyous, sobbing embrace better suited to a couple reuniting after a war than to a husband and wife buying radicchio in the produce aisle.

If a man has the sense that God gave a common bivalve—and I often wonder if those clams know something we don't—he should realize when he's found a partner who complements him, makes him happy, and vice versa. Because the right person isn't solely someone who's happy with you, it's also someone who's not afraid to be unhappy with you. There's no such thing as a perfect couple. Anyone who claims otherwise is either drunk, on Ecstasy, lying, or all three, and—bet on it—has at some point imagined crushing his or her spouse with a giant suitcase or some other large, blunt object. But if you can refrain from doing it, and eventually laugh about it, you're making out OK.

Still standing on the bridge, I removed a 500-lire piece from my pocket, made a wish, flicked the gold-and-silver coin into the dark water below, and hurried back to the apartment, where I saw that my wish had come true: Celia was still there.

**WORKERS**

# STAY AT HOME, DAD

CHARLIE LEDUFF

BEFORE MY DAUGHTER WAS BORN, men my age—colleagues and other acquaintances—were happy to ladle out unsolicited advice about becoming a father. I would come to find that it wasn't advice at all, but rather superficial observation, masculine lip gloss about what it feels like to be the Male Influence. I would realize how little they knew about their children.

What they told me ranged from the obvious to the disturbing:

"For the first six months, they're pretty much just digestive tracts," said one friend, whom I shall call Mr. Unhappy.

"It's the most meaningful thing that will ever happen to you," said Mr. Oprah's Book Club.

"To tell you the truth, I can't wait to go to work in the morning," said Mr. Saddest of Them All.

Of course, five days a week these men pack off and dutifully trudge to desks somewhere, though a few of them aren't necessarily chained to those desks. These lucky sorts of men are writers for big, important, sometimes meaningful publications. And from my perspective, sitting here in Los Angeles at noon, still in my underpants, such a man may be the most envied creature in all of manhood.

I imagine him now, off in the bush, meeting with an aggrieved group of rebels. Or he is carousing in the streets of a European capital, drinking good wine with a minister of something or other. Or he is beating it across a border with a group of barefoot migrants. He could be anywhere, meditating over a body of water, bewitched by the lights of an exotic city.

Wherever he may be, I am consumed with him and his adventures. You see, I was once one of his species, a jet-set correspondent for the *New York Times*. I'd be in the Arctic watching Eskimos prepare for a whale hunt one week and drinking beer with a Mexican smuggler the next.

Now I am another creature altogether. I am a stay-at-home dad.

Allow me a qualification here. It is a blessing to watch your baby's eyes—those fluttering, little half-moons—slowly transform from slate to brown. The eyebrows grow in later, in case you did not know. There is the moment when the little beast has figured out how to stand on her wobbly legs with the help of a chair. These are the good parts.

But I am a man, and a man at home alone with an infant is up the hill without a rope. Confusion reigns. How much to feed? How much sleep? When? The baby does not know. You do not know. Those baby books are confusing, long-winded, and in need of some good editing. The little thing howls, flushes crimson, gasps for air. You grow frightened. Fear gives way to weariness. Then, like a heel, you close the door and walk away.

My go-to-work wife returns home after I've endured nine hours of this, nine hours of my cleaning toilets and ruining clothes and washing Claudette's diapers and mopping floors. When my go-to-work wife walks in the door thirty minutes late, I'm there to ask where her priorities are. It's the stuff of daytime talk shows.

How did I come to raise a baby? It was simple, really. My wife was alone for months at a time while I was scampering around Iraq or Mexico or working on an investigative piece about a slaughterhouse. While I was out for late-night cocktails, accepting prizes, speaking at universities, she was studying child psychology—of all things—and working small jobs and never complaining.

Then, a month after our baby was born, she got a job offer. What were we to do? My job at the *Times* was wearing thin. I could feel it, like the last days in the palace of Haile Selassie. The baby had come unexpectedly early, while I was across the continent working on a story. The job owned me, and I was sick of it. I resigned. No leave of absence. No severance package. No gold watch. And off my lady went on her career.

Becoming a stay-at-home dad seemed noble from the romantic distance of a boy with two stepfathers. Stay-at-home dad—why not? We are an older couple who'd been waiting a long time for a baby to come, and now that she had, what were we to do? Fob her off on a stranger before she had taken her first step?

They say the number of stay-at-home fathers in America has doubled in the last decade, but I would venture to guess that this has more to do with a shaky labor market than it does with a mass flowering of male compassion. It was never a dream of mine to raise a baby, and sometimes, when the baby's asleep, I find myself staring into the rearview mirror of my career. There was that time in Iraq when I wandered into a city hall taken over by a radical cleric and his followers. Me, the Catholic. They, the Muslims. It was Good Friday, and in the spirit of brotherhood we prayed together. By the end, the holy man's supporters were chanting with thumbs raised high: "Charlie good! Charlie good!" In some way I was an ambassador that day, an American armed with only a pen.

Every year, in early September, I get phone calls. I got one the other day, in fact. It was a tough man with tears in his throat thanking me for the work I had done during those dark days at Ground Zero, thanking me for writing his name down for posterity. You're welcome, Bobby.

As a reporter, your job is to write about history as it is happening, so our grandchildren know how we lived. The reporter gives people things to talk about. He rubs elbows with and makes suggestions to people in power and exposes the wrongs they do. He holds up a mirror to society, going where few would, asking questions few dare. He is the arbiter of what is interesting. That is power.

That is what this stay-at-home dad would tell his old self.

I also would tell him that once he stops being a reporter, the governor won't call anymore. Neither will the old colleagues. There will be no more Hollywood parties. No expense account. No action.

It will be just you and the kid. And the kid will have no idea how good you were. And worse, in the mania of your empty house and isolated by the Los Angeles car culture, when the afternoon sun is bright and debilitating and that old deadline time, that hour of adrenaline, is upon you, right about then you will wonder whether you were really any good at all. You will find yourself staring into a dirty diaper as though it were tea leaves, trying to augur some story about the failings of the latest immigration bill.

· · · ·

You might say we are in the early stages of a love story, my daughter and I. Her first words were either "kitty, kitty" or "Hi, Daddy." I'm not sure which, but it doesn't matter. I taught them to her, and I was there to hear them. When she falls or bangs her head, she cries it out and then crawls on about her business. Resiliency—I am teaching her that. She likes people, and people are attracted to her lumpy smile and flailing arms, and this makes me hopeful for her future. She pulls hair at the playground, and we're working to correct that. She takes naps on my chest.

The go-to-work man loves his baby too, of course, sometimes more than his job. He loves the little one from 6 p.m. to 9 p.m. and during the Saturday trip to the petting zoo. He loves her from the time he removes his jacket to the time he pours himself a Scotch and then all throughout his dinner. He changes a diaper perhaps, pats the dumpling on the head, and gives her a good-night kiss. If he has a more intense job, go-to-work dad arrives home at 7 or 8 or 9 p.m. or next week or maybe next month. My wife reminds me that if I had kept my power job, I would be watching the little one grow up through pictures on my cell phone.

I am sad for those fathers I knew during the years of my power job. I remember the soldier in Iraq who was not there for the birth of his child; the journalist who came back from the war zone only to be called Uncle by his son; the Mexican man on Long Island whose only presence back home was his photograph and a Western Union receipt. I feel sadness for the man who lost his son because of a wayward bomb; the father whose son was snatched away in the middle of the night by Saddam's secret police; the father whose son died when a skyscraper collapsed on him one unseasonably warm September morning.

I was mulling this over one workday morning as I drove my daughter to a Mommy and Me yoga class. "I'm sorry," the nasally male clerk behind the desk said when we arrived at the studio.

"Sorry about what?" I asked.

"The class is closed."

"The class is closed?"

"Yes," he stammered. "Closed, uh, well, closed . . ."

"What are you trying to say? Closed to me because I'm not a mommy?"

"I'm afraid so. Some women might not feel comfortable with you in there."

I left without incident. Why shouldn't women have a club where they can be free from the stink of testosterone? No woman wants to reveal her sagging parts, her leaking parts, her postnatal pimples to the male interloper. I could have made a scene about the unfairness of it, the double standard, the fact that the golf clubs and fraternal orders have been pried open by women in the name of equality.

I could whine on about how, during the birthing classes and pre-natal checkup appointments, the man is considered slightly more than a nuisance—a damp dog, more or less. "What?" the doctor said as I tried to articulate the emotional difficulties that I, the man, was having with "being pregnant." She acted as though she did not hear a word I said, as though her misplaced paper clip needing tending to first.

"Never mind."

I left to put coins in the parking meter, thinking, "Be a man, for god's sake."

The feelings of the homebound male range from self-pity to joy. I'm told that women have similar struggles. Who is she when she becomes a mother? Is she who she once was? Will she ever be anything more? Beats me.

As the baby and I left Yoga World, I was thinking I really ought to be working. I wondered what country my friend Mike was in that day. What glorious trouble might he be getting himself into? Does Mike do yoga?

We went off to the park to see my new friends, the Latina nannies who care for the Little Lord Fauntleroys of Los Angeles. This is a park for the upper-middle class. It is on the edge of a neighborhood with enormous, early-twentieth-century Craftsman homes. It is a fifteen-minute walk from my working-class neighborhood, but it is another city altogether. Strivers live here, people who crave the lawn, the prestige, the German car. So both parents go off to fulfill themselves; and off the babies go, with the nanny or to day care.

The price of striving can be steep. As my nanny friend Angelica puts it, "The children love us more than they love their parents. The little one calls me Mommy."

I am determined that my child will not call someone other than me Papa. And so we run our little routine: breakfast, nap, walk, church, park, lunch, nap, bath, book time, toy time, Mommy time, dinner, bed, and then a nice glass of Pinot for Papa.

Still, the ennui must show like welts. An older man in my neighborhood, Jose, offered me an observation one day without prompting. It was so penetrating, I wrote it down: "The whole world is in your *brazos* there, amigo. That little girl is your world and your future and your blood. That is your hair and your eyes I can see. A man, if he is truly a man, does what God asks him to do, to honor his family."

"I know this, *Tío*," I said, fascinated that he could decipher me from across a street. "But it is hard sometimes for me to be happy about it."

"Ah, you are a traveler? And sometimes you see this duty of yours as women's work?"

"Yes," I said. "I think they must be better at it."

"This does not matter," he told me. "You must be better. If not the woman, then the man, yes? This is preferable to the stranger, who is not truly able to give the child love."

He said it just like that. Jose articulated the true point—the nut graph, they call it in journalism—the thing my friends, the go-to-work dads, could not or were unwilling to tell me: You have to decide whether the child is more important to you than the stature, the action, the laurels, the money. If she is, then you must accept it and get on with the dreary business of the routine.

．．．．

My daughter is awake now. She is standing in her crib, her arms out. I'm still in my underpants. "Hi, Daddy," she clucks. Or maybe it's "kitty, kitty." It doesn't matter, really. She is talking to me. I know I will return to work someday. We could use the money, and honestly, I need a place in my life that belongs to me. Right now my life is here, but eventually I'll find new places to go.

I already know that day will be a sad one. It will be the day my daughter will not need her father so much anymore, and perhaps by then, her father will not need her so very much either.

# SHOOTING THE TRUTH

MICHAEL KAMBER

MY FATHER LEFT IN 1969, when I was six and he was forty-five. He got a VW microbus, a nineteen-year-old blonde, and started making up for time lost on the three kids and the drunkard wife back in Maine. He was chasing hard after the tail end of the '60s. I always supposed it must have been a tough time for a man to be tied down—watching all that chaos out there, while having to stay home and diaper the kids and pay the bills.

He left a few things behind: some tools, a handful of war medals, and a fantastically detailed lithograph he'd bought at a yard sale. It was dated 1918 and called *Over the Top*. It showed a company of steely-eyed doughboys storming a trench, their bayonets fixed and the flag waving above them. The Germans looked scared and slightly evil in their pointy helmets. One American was falling, looking skyward as his comrades killed the Huns around him.

I used to stare at the print for hours, studying it as if it were a religious talisman, searching the images—the smoke from the cannons, the charging soldiers, the blood dripping from men's bodies—for some clue I'd missed. These men had the answer to a question I wanted to ask. I just wasn't sure what the question was. I wanted to know why men go to distant places to slaughter one another, and how that becomes something noble. But there was a deeper question beyond that.

Some of the medals my father left behind were from the First World War. They had belonged to his father, my grandfather, Bob Kamber. The most beautiful of his medals was a rainbow-colored campaign ribbon with brass bars inscribed with the names of the battles he'd fought in: St. Mihiel, Meuse-Argonne, Aisne Marne, Belleau Wood. I used to run my fingers over the names like a blind man reading Braille.

My father also fought, in the Second World War, with the 5th Marines. He celebrated his twentieth birthday in the volcanic ash of Iwo Jima. I had his medals, too, and a tattered fatigue jacket with a front pocket bearing the Marine Corps logo—the globe nestled on a rope and an anchor.

My grandfather hung out at the VFW and was a proud member of the Disabled American Veterans. But he never talked about the combat, and neither did my father. If I asked, they gave vague responses.

My father never really fit in anywhere. He fought his way through life, never held a job for long, ran through four marriages (one before my mother and two after), surrounded himself with guns, occasionally threatened other men—"I'm an ex-marine, you know." It was only later, after I'd been to war, that I began to wonder, Did he live with things he'd seen that never went away?

. . . .

My daughter was born when I was nineteen. I was building transmissions in a small shop in Asbury Park, New Jersey, during the day and working in a restaurant at night. There was a waitress there with blonde hair and a tight uniform. I got her pregnant one night in the backseat of my '67 Mustang. A few months after my daughter was born, I was in the supermarket buying Pampers and formula when I ran into my boys. They were buying beer for a night on the town.

I was ashamed I wasn't out chasing women and getting drunk. I felt I'd failed a vision of manhood that I'd inherited, both as my father's son and simply as an American male. I'd lost my independence to roam, to seduce women, and, most important, to inflict or endure violence.

I contemplated going to Mexico, like I'd seen guys in the movies do, just running someplace where no one knew me and I could get a clean start. But I'd never been farther west than Ohio, so I stuck it out in New Jersey and slept on my girlfriend's mom's couch, until the mother, seeing I wasn't going to marry her daughter, threw me out.

I did raise my daughter, after a fashion. She stayed with me on weekends and for a month or two in the summer, and got my phone calls from the road. I put her through college and grad school. I learned from my grandfather that you work hard and you take a certain amount of responsibility.

In all fairness to my father, he tried to keep in touch when I was young. It didn't help that my mother had a warrant out for him. In my teens I lived with him for a time, but he was a violent, bitter man, and we fought constantly. The day after graduating from high school, I was gone.

I never set out to cover wars. I saved some money at the transmission shop and went to art school in New York to be a fine art photographer. My daughter and her mom stayed behind in New Jersey; my daughter's mom still waitresses in the same restaurant where I met her twenty-five years ago. I dropped out of school when the money ran out, and I started trying to make it as a photojournalist—a job where I could combine my love for photography with my fascination with history. I worked construction during the week, then shot on the streets of New York at night and on weekends, peddling pictures to the wire services for twenty-five dollars apiece.

In 1987, when I was twenty-four, a friend was going to Haiti to cover the first election after the fall of "Baby Doc" Duvalier and invited me along. A community newspaper in New York gave me credentials and a promise to give my work a look when I returned. I went with my friend and accidentally made it to war, but it didn't look like the picture on the wall in Maine. There were no battle lines, no armies in uniforms. On a steaming November morning, I found myself in a room full of women and girls who'd been hacked to death with machetes by Duvalier's thugs.

Later that morning, those thugs, the Tonton Macoutes, caught me out in the street, photographing a fresh corpse like it was some sort of anthropological experiment. I knew what that deeper question was now. A few minutes ago, this man was alive, breathing, going home to his family, working on his dreams for tomorrow. Now he lay dead on the pavement. I wanted to know why. I thought my camera might reveal an answer, but I had lingered too long. The killers trained their guns on me, talked for a moment, and then drove away. Other journalists were killed that day. I was spared. For days afterward I shook so badly I couldn't pick up a glass of water; sleep eluded me for months.

I've covered a dozen wars since then. I manage it better now, but that feeling of absolute, heart-pounding terror never goes away. In Iraq, near An Nāsirīyah or Mosul, we would drive down a dirt road where, a day or two before, a Humvee had blown up; we would see bodies being carried out in small pieces. You knew the insurgents had been out at night setting new IEDs—improvised explosive devices—and so you'd sweat and clench and swear you'll never do this again. If you can just make it through this time, you promise, you'll never come back. Then you turn around and do it again the next day or the next week, and you can't explain why.

Some men think it's bravery. John Burns, the Baghdad bureau chief for the *New York Times*, once told me that much of what is termed bravery is simply men being too obstinate, or too dumb, to understand their own mortality. I don't know what it is for me, but I sometimes feel as if I'm standing on a beach and there are waves smothering me—waves of advertisements for shit I don't need, of profiles of people who've never done anything except be famous, of politicians mouthing platitudes, of hundreds of TV channels showing nothing. And sometimes I can take one picture that lets me grab onto something real in this world.

· · · ·

Not long ago in Iraq, I walked into the countryside in the dawn light
with a platoon of U.S. soldiers. Most were in their early twenties; a few
were only eighteen or nineteen years old. They had joined the army for
many reasons, some out of patriotism, some—the ones from military
families—because that's just what you did at eighteen, some because
they wanted to prove themselves and loved the action and camarade-
rie. They were a cocky, cheerful bunch. They told fag jokes and stories
about getting pissed together, about bar fights and getting so drunk
they ate one another's puke.

On patrol that morning, the commander paused for a long moment
to get map coordinates and do radio checks. Then we set off along
a sandy trail that wended through a handful of bombed-out houses.
The air was still, and in the palm groves beyond the trail there was an
early-morning beauty that I'd never seen before in Iraq, a place I would
rate as the most unlovely of the fifty or so countries I've worked in.
Still, I felt uneasy on the trail. The sand was good cover for an IED or
a command-detonated mine, and the palm groves offered excellent
cover for snipers.

I stepped inside an abandoned building to photograph the patrol
through a shattered window. Birds chirped in the distance as I studied
the rubble for trip wires. And then *whoomph!* The air filled with smoke.
Shrapnel rained down around me. A soldier screamed. I checked my legs
and the rest of my body for wounds. Had I tripped an IED? Was I dead
and didn't know it? There was no blood. A feeling of nausea settled
over me. I'd heard the sound of an explosion often enough before. It
comes at the moment of a man's death. I knew I had to go out there and
start shooting.

I ran through the smoke, listening for gunfire—a sign of an
ongoing attack—but there was none. A call went out alerting us that
we might be in a minefield. No one moved except me and the medic.

Through the haze I saw an eight-foot-wide crater, and behind it,
a soldier's upper torso. He'd been cut in half above the waist. His legs
were gone and his eyes were open, staring at the sky. His blood pooled
slowly in the sand. Behind him the medic was already at work on another
bloody soldier. I raised my camera and started to shoot.

"No fucking pictures!" the captain screamed. Soldiers have gotten violent with me when their comrades have been killed. I took a few frames then put the camera down and started helping to bandage the most badly wounded soldier. He had taken a lot of shrapnel, and his face looked like hamburger. We checked his torso for wounds, but there were none. He was pleading, "Doc, you got to give me something. I can't take this pain. I can't take it." His friend was lying dead against his legs, but he didn't know it. He couldn't see through the blood in his eyes, and he felt nothing but the stabbing pain.

The scene was eerily quiet, save for a radioman calling for a medevac. A minute later, the soldier's sobbing began to mix with the birdcalls in the stifling, still air.

I slowly walked over to the captain and told him that I was going to do my job and that he could take my cameras later if he wanted. He nodded to me, maybe knowing that no one was going to move through a minefield to stop me anyway. I walked among the wounded men, shooting as I went and trying to lend a hand where I could. Platoon members carefully put the wounded onto litters and carried them to a landing zone for the helos. Then four young men lifted the dead soldier's torso gently into a body bag. One bent down and began to rip the gear off his comrade's flak vest. Then he thought better of it, reached up, and quietly zipped the bag closed.

Another platoon, working a few hundred meters to the south of us, had a soldier sniped through the brain a few minutes later. They evac'd him with his helmet still on, to keep his head from falling apart. He died an hour or so later.

No one saw the enemy in either attack. The war in Iraq is bad that way. Mostly, you ride around as IED bait instead of engaging the enemy. But I bet the boys in the trenches thought World War I was a shitty war, too. I wonder what the lithograph from this war will look like. It's hard to make a heroic picture of guys slogging through the fields, fearing, expecting, waiting for an ambush.

· · · ·

I had a plan when I was in Iraq. I was going to come back to the States and live on a tree-lined street with this smart, sexy woman I loved.

She had an apartment full of sunlight. Our friends and family would be there with us, eating and laughing.

But when I returned to Brooklyn, something had changed, in me and in the city. In my formerly industrial neighborhood, black nannies now pushed fat white babies in $400 strollers; my neighbor's new car had separate air-conditioning zones for each occupant; a friend obsessed over his iPod remote control. No one was the least concerned with the Iraq war. My neighbors' programs did not include getting their legs or testicles blown off by someone wiring 155-millimeter shells together and pressing a garage door opener. They didn't worry about having to shit into a colostomy bag, or about being spoon-fed because they had gotten their arms blown off. And why should they?

So I got back to the world and I felt a certain arrogance washing over me, and a certain anger. I couldn't think about much except getting out again. My woman wanted me to go into therapy, but I didn't feel the need to pay an expert to facilitate this intersection—the intersection between the violence I saw every day in Iraq and people going blithely about their lives at home. And I wasn't going to cop to this war junkie stuff.

I'd found a useful role in this world, a way to give evidence that has value. I had nothing to apologize for, nothing I needed to be diagnosed for. Some things in this world just are, and that's all right. They don't need to be satisfactorily resolved.

I put my things in storage and took the first assignment that got me far from New York.

I leave for the Congo next week, then for Iraq again in a couple of months—it will be the fifth calendar year in which I've worked there. I have no home really, just the road, a room in Baghdad, a few friends' places in Dakar where I sometimes crash.

I'm forty-five now, the same age my father was when he split, and maybe I'm not that different from him. I know my limitations better. Unlike him, I got out before I got in. But his fascination with violence, his need to stay in motion, and his desire to be irresponsible have all filtered down into me. And I'm OK with that.

# BLOOD-SPATTERED

JULIO MEDINA

I SHUFFLED INTO the Albany County courthouse, cuffed and shackled, to hear my sentence. My mom was there with my brothers and sisters. I was twenty-five at the time and the leader of a drug gang that included ten other people. The judge read my crimes: nine counts of conspiracy and various other offenses related to the hand grenades and the cache of machine guns the police had found. While the judge read, I ignored the reporters and cameras—it was a big case—and everyone else in the courtroom and looked at my mom. I saw her turn to my brothers and sisters and ask, "Who the hell is this guy they're talking about?" I still get chills remembering the look on her face when she finally figured out the guy they were talking about was me. I was sentenced to seven years to life.

In prison it took a while for it to sink in, for me to realize that I belonged there, that this wasn't a mistake. The first place they put me was Comstock, in upstate New York, probably one of the dirtiest, filthiest prisons there is. Rats ran back and forth on the bars all the time. We had to hang our food on the ceiling, and they'd still jump at it like trapeze artists. One day I was doing push-ups when a rat ran right over my back.

I eventually got transferred to Sing Sing, the most violent prison in the country. The corrections officers would search you before you went into the mess halls. They would throw you up against a wall and pat you down. One time when I was being searched I looked at this particular corrections officer, and he looked at me. I just nodded my head and went into the hall to eat. Afterward, this same guy came down to my cell.

"Yo, how're you doing?" he asked.

"I'm good, man," I said. "How're you?"

"As you can see, I'm a corrections officer now."

Then I recognized him. We grew up together in the projects. I was the godfather to his son. When we were eighteen, we robbed a bank together. He had gotten a job as a teller, and we arranged for me to come into the bank at a certain time, stick a gun in his face, and ask for all the money he had in his drawer. Afterward we split the take. But we got caught.

Seeing him made me think about how small a difference there can be between who goes to prison and who becomes a guard. It just depends on some decisions and choices we make.

• • • •

I grew up in the South Bronx, the poorest area in the country at that time—not that it's an excuse. Mom worked two, three jobs, and she drank. I'd come into the apartment sometimes and find her lying on the floor and I'd carry her to the bedroom.

I met my father only two or three times, when I made it back to Puerto Rico. Mom left there before I was born, to escape him; he once tried to run her over with a car. But when I was ten, Mom sent me to

Puerto Rico to see him because she thought I needed to know who my dad was. When we met, two other men were with him. I didn't know who they were. Before getting out of his car, my dad reached into his glove compartment, took out a long gun, and put it underneath his coat. We walked around a shopping mall with these two guys, who, I finally realized, were his bodyguards. I saw my father again more recently, about five years ago. We talked briefly, no more than eight minutes. He couldn't have cared less about me, and that fucking tore me up.

In my projects in the South Bronx there were no attorneys or doctors, but there were drug dealers and pimps. Those were the guys I looked up to, the ones I wanted to be like. I did grow up with Tiny Archibald, who went on to play for the Boston Celtics, but I couldn't play basketball, so that limited my options. The drug dealers had the cars, gave us tickets to the Apollo Theater, bought us brand-new baseball bats and gloves. We'd go to the park and play baseball with the stuff they gave us. We all thought they were so cool. I didn't know they were killing people as part of their businesses.

My initial rite of passage was when I got my first package of drugs and sold them. I was fourteen years old then, and I was able to bring food into the house and take care of my family. I went to Catholic school. I even went to college at the state university at Albany, but I went there mostly for business. In Albany I was the college pharmacist; those kids had more money than my customers in the Bronx.

School wasn't for me. I wasn't going to be a social worker and make $25,000 a year. I was determined to do better than that, but I channeled that energy in the wrong direction. I was arrested at fifteen, at sixteen, at eighteen. And then at twenty, I was sentenced to two and a half years for possessing and selling drugs. I was sent to a minimum-security camp.

At the camp, there were a lot of Colombians, a lot of Dominicans, who were serving short sentences. We were all making plans on how to get rich when we got out. I set up my whole organization right there. These guys would get the drugs from South America, and I would distribute the drugs. At the camp I taught myself the craft of drug dealing. I learned how to be the leader of a big-time drug gang.

. . . .

In Sing Sing, my cell was so small that I could stand in the middle of it and touch both walls. Those walls were metal, so in the summer it got really hot in the cells. Most days it was 120 degrees. When the guards walked by, that was my air-conditioning—that little breeze they made. They sold little fans for the cells, but I refused to buy one. I wanted to feel every fucking day of that prison sentence.

I wanted to remember every time how, after my family came to visit me, I was strip searched, how I was dehumanized. After leaving my mother, I'd have to stand totally naked while a guard ran his fingers through my mouth and then my hair. He'd lift my nut sack, make sure there was nothing underneath, and then put my hands behind my ears, turn me around, and say, "Bottom of the left foot, bottom of the right foot. Uh oh, I didn't see that left foot. Now move your toes around." I would have to stand on one fucking leg, trying to balance, until this asshole decided to tell me to put my leg down. Then he'd tell me to spread them. I'd bend over so he could see in my asshole. He'd say, "I didn't see that." So I'd spread them again. I remember all this—vividly.

Even after I went to prison, my family worshipped me. They treated me as if I were a political prisoner or something. I had supported them when I was out, and to them I was still the head of the family. Then one day my favorite niece—this beautiful young woman who I adored—visited me at Sing Sing. She told me about her boyfriend, how she was so proud of him and how much I would like him. She couldn't stop talking about this guy. I called home that night and talked to my sister, her mom. She told me that the boyfriend was the biggest drug dealer in New York, and that's why I would like him. That shit hit me like a ton of bricks. I vowed right then that I'd never sell another drug. Even if I had to eat rocks and shovel shit when I got out, I was not going to be that guy anymore.

A year later, in my fifth year in Sing Sing, just after I turned thirty, I enrolled in a master's degree program that the New York Theological Seminary ran at the prison. I got into the program thinking it might help me get out of prison—it would look good to the parole board. But the program gave me the tools to recognize I was more than a drug dealer.

I'm a social dude. I can talk to African-Americans, Latinos, whites; I can transcend barriers that a lot of people can't. The seminary allowed me to see that as a drug dealer, I made millions of dollars, had homes, traveled the world, but that my real gift as a dealer was that I knew my community. I could assess it. So why not assess the community to see what's wrong with it and try to make positive changes?

I started thinking about what I could do even while I was still in prison. Sing Sing is all long-timers, lifers, gangbangers, so there's constant violence. When somebody's going to be stabbed, you move out of the way. You don't want to get any blood on you because if you do, you have two options: talk and then get killed by another inmate, or be put in the box for not talking. So when someone was stabbed, you didn't react with concern for this other human being. Instead you might say, "Oh God, you got stabbed, and now the blood is on me, so now they're going to question me. You asshole!" He's bleeding to death, and you're mad at him because the stabbing took place close to you.

One day, after I started going to the seminary, I was walking toward the chapel when up ahead of me a guy got stabbed really badly. Everybody just kept walking. "It ain't none of your business," someone said. Guys were jumping over the body and the pool of blood. When I got to the man he was bleeding out onto the floor and, I swear to God, I could not walk over that blood. It was like something was pushing me to look at this man, look at what was happening here. Guys were like, "Yo! Yo!" But I could not move. All I could do is say, "This shit has to stop."

The guys looked at me like I was crazy; at one time I was involved in half the stabbings at the prison. They started swearing at me, saying, "What the hell are you talking about?"

I said it again: "This just has to stop, man. We have to stop killing one another."

Everything changed for me at that moment. Finances didn't matter anymore. It didn't matter if I traveled around the country, or if I could do whatever. It didn't matter. It was like, how do I not help people? How do I not stop and look at the humanity in each person, man? How do I recognize that these are all God's children, man? And how do we become part of that human family so that we don't kill each other?

I got the guy up off the ground and got his blood spattered all over me. The guards came running to us and got me out of the way. They didn't question me because they saw what I had done. They thought I was crazy for helping this guy.

. . . .

After the stabbing, I started organizing gang interventions in the prison. We got permission from the warden to hang signs saying, "We love you, Daddy," from the children whose fathers were in prison. In the hallway where most of the stabbings took place, the one on the way to the chapel, we hung posters with kids' handprints and their fathers' handprints on top of them. The posters had a great impact.

I dedicated my life to stopping the violence in prison, getting to the young people who are hard to talk to. They'd tell me, "We don't want to hear this Martin Luther King shit again." I'd say, "Brother, just give me a shot here, man." I wasn't preachy or talking about God or anything. I mostly listened and asked: "How do we change our reality, man? How do we make the best of our time here, man? How do we come out whole, if that's possible? And how do we take care of our families and make sure that they don't look at us and mimic our behavior?"

. . . .

Getting out of prison after fifteen years was the tough part. I was well-off prior to prison. I had gotten rich off the drug trade. Now I was living with my mother for the first time since I was sixteen, in a tiny apartment. My brother was living there, too, and he was still getting high.

My old friends came by. They drove up to the front of my building in these nice cars, and my mother watched from the terrace, nervous.

"Hey, what's up guys? How you doing?" I asked them.

"Come on, man, let's go," one of them said to me.

"No, I'm not going anywhere."

"What d'you mean? You know, we've been waiting for you!"

"Well then, you waited for the wrong guy if you were waiting for me, man. That guy died in prison."

I didn't want to go back to selling drugs, but I couldn't find a job. I went on interview after interview after interview after interview. My girl was working, my mother worked. I was the only one in the house not working. I would paint something in the house just to try to contribute somehow. On the job interviews, everyone would ask me where I'd been during the last year. I just made things up. After three months I finally got a job, as a substance abuse counselor.

 During my job search I decided that what I really wanted to do was help my brothers coming out of prison. I had earned a master's degree, and I thought I had enough social skills to get work, but no one would hire me. I was one of the smartest guys coming out, so I couldn't imagine what would happen to my boys who didn't have GEDs and could barely read or write. I don't mean to put my brothers down, but it's pretty easy to be at the top of the heap in Sing Sing. Fifty percent of the convicted can't read or write, and 20 percent of them are diagnosed with a mental-health issue, and I would say a lot more go undiagnosed. When I got turned down for jobs over and over again, the reality hit me: "Shit, if I'm having a hard time, what about those dudes I left behind?"

Just after I started my new job, one of my closest, closest friends came to me and said, "It's time, now. We got to get to Washington. We have all these different deals happening in different states, and I need you to help me coordinate what's going on."

I told him, "I can't do that, man. I don't have the heart. That's just not who I am."

He put his hands in my face and said, "You're a punk." He pushed my face harder and harder. "And you're a faggot. I knew it, man. I knew you were soft."

He's a tough guy, and I was a tough guy—two elephants looking at each other, flaring. He was getting to me. I was very close to letting anger get the better of me, but then I saw something deep in his eyes. He wished he could change positions with me. That's what I saw. *You got a second chance, Julio, to start off differently, man. I don't have that chance. I'm entrenched in this thing.* He would love to be in my rinky-dink suit, with my ten-dollar shoes from Payless and my funny tie, in my shitty little office. I saw that this was a smart guy, a very smart guy, who was trapped.

We never spoke again, but seeing him helped me realize how many other people want to be out of that life. You're so steeped in it—your whole life has been based around selling drugs and other crimes—that there's no way out. It's no accident that 40 percent of inmates who get out end up back in prison within six months.

• • • •

As soon as I got out, guys from Sing Sing started writing me and sending me their résumés, asking me what I thought of them. After work, I would sit down at my mother's kitchen table and rework their résumés and write them letters telling them what they needed to do, what they needed to say. The onslaught of letters and résumés kept coming, kept coming, and I would ask myself, "Who's out here to get people really prepared?"

In the letters I'd get questions like, "My wife's been living without me for 10 years, how am I going to be able to contribute?" Or "Hey Julio, I was 16 when I went to prison. I'm 35 now. I'm a virgin; the only relationships I've had were with other men, so I don't know where I am sexually." There wasn't a place for them to talk about any of that. There wasn't a place for them to ask, "Yo man, I grew up in prison. I grew up in institutions. How do I make this adjustment out here?"

So ten years ago I walked away from my job and created Exodus. Call it faith, because I had no job, no money. I walked away because it was my calling. We now have 500 former inmates coming through our program every year. We teach life skills so my brothers and sisters can become productive members of society and don't end up back in prison. Exodus helps inmates adjust to being fathers and sons, husbands and wives, good friends and neighbors on the outside. We help former inmates find and keep a job to support themselves, restore their dignity, and avoid resorting to crime.

I also teach at Sing Sing, in the same program I graduated from. I've met the president and senators, music and sports stars over these last ten years. PBS made a documentary about our program, *Hard Road Home*. But my greatest honor is to go back and teach the inmates, so I can show these men that they can change their lives.

My life changed that day I got blood on my prison uniform. God intervened that day. There was a hand on me. I wasn't crazy. I wasn't using drugs. I was in my right mind. A hand stopped me, and something said to me, you cannot cross over your brother's blood.

# KHAN WITHOUT THE WRATH

CURTIS B.

FRIDAY NIGHT in Mongolia's Bulgan City was like the Wild West meeting the twenty-first century. Men would ride their horses through town—right alongside the cars—tie them up to fence posts, and go into the bars. They'd get drunk and eventually a couple of them would piss each other off and box it out with bare knuckles—no guns, no knives; that was bitch to them. "Who fights with guns and knives?" they'd say if anyone asked. "That's not how Genghis Khan did it, and that's not how we're going to do it."

Typically during one of these Friday-night fistfights, one of the guys would fall, his face all bloody. Then he'd pull himself back up, and he and the guy he'd been fighting would share another bottle of vodka, hop on their horses, and head home. The Mongolians were big, burly people, and they would say to me, a kid from an East Coast inner city, "You guys are big. Why don't you fight like we do? Why do you shoot each other?"

Back home, just a couple of months ago, one of my cousins was shot and nearly paralyzed in a gunfight. Another was shot up in a car. My uncle Earl got shot a few years back. My uncle Harley was defending his mother in their own home when he got shot. My cousins walk around with guns. That's the reality of the neighborhoods where I grew up.

Killing did play a part in the Mongolians' concept of manhood: If you could kill a sheep or a goat, and dress it, you were considered a man, even if you were only twelve years old. When you could kill animals you became the breadwinner of your family. You were strong, and you were reliable.

· · · ·

For the first three months I was in the Peace Corps, I lived with a host family in Ulaanbaatar, the capital of Mongolia. Then one day a Peace Corps official told me, "We're proud of you. You made it to your three months. You're now fluent in Russian and Mongolian. We think you know how to survive. So here's $200, here's the city you're going to be in, and here's your apartment. We'll see you next year." Or words to that effect.

Bulgan was in the middle of a country on the other side of the world with a culture I still knew nothing about. A lot of people had a postcard image of what their Peace Corps experience would be like, and when it wasn't like that, they crumbled; they gave up. I didn't give up.

I lived in a Soviet-era apartment. It was a couple hundred square feet and made of concrete, which was constantly crumbling. I had a toilet but no hot water. I had to wash clothes by hand. I didn't have a refrigerator for two years. In the summer I'd take the top off the toilet tank, and when I had beer or milk I would drop it into the water tank to keep it cold. During the winter, I would buy extra meat at the market— they would kill the food right in front of you and then give you your slab—and I'd put plastic wrap all over it and then hang it outside and let it freeze. It got to about –20° Celsius there. By December, the whole country was a freezer.

My first day in Bulgan, I watched the TV that the Peace Corps had given me. It was small and old, and the one channel that came in consistently showed nothing but European fashion programs. I hadn't showered for two weeks and I felt like shit, but I could watch Italian supermodels all day. I watched the TV because it was the only way I could hear English and listen to music I recognized.

. . . .

My grandmother raised my sister and me. Our mom passed away when I was two and my sister was just a baby. My dad was an absent figure. In that regard, we were hardly a novelty in the inner-city neighborhoods where I grew up. When I was eight years old, Grandma had an epiphany. She knew that I needed a male role model in my life. But she didn't see any good ones around. My uncles and cousins were in and out of jail, or they were local hustlers. Grandma really wanted to steer me away from that life.

A social worker introduced us to Big Brothers, and that's how I met Tim. All I knew was the inner city. I had never seen a white face before, besides my social worker's. So when they introduced me to Tim, I said, "Who the hell is this white dude, and what does he want?" I had asked for Michael Jordan or someone like him, and instead I got this young white guy wanting to be my friend.

Tim had just graduated from college and was working for a bank. We spent a lot of time together, and he helped me see there was more to the world than just what I saw in the 'hood. When he got married, he asked me to be his best man. When my grandmother passed away, I went to live with Tim and his wife, Maureen, in a wealthy, almost all-white suburb, to finish high school. I went to college and then taught kindergarten for a while and worked on John Kerry's presidential campaign. But I knew what I really wanted to do was join the Peace Corps. It was something I felt I had to do.

. . . .

Bulgan City had a population of about 12,000. By Mongolian standards, that's big. There were no paved roads in the countryside, so it took two hours to travel twenty-four miles to the next town. The first time I went to the bank in Bulgan, I felt as if I was in the movie *The Matrix*. The place was bustling, but as soon as I walked in, everything froze. People just stopped and looked at me. But after a while, once the Mongolians got over the weirdness of having me in their community, they were actually very open. People would invite me to their houses for dinner; they would teach me how to make a fire, how to kill animals. But I knew to draw the line when it came to having relationships with their women. That was dicey politics that I chose to stay away from. I ended up with a Swiss schoolteacher.

I was a community youth development volunteer, working with young adults and kids as young as five. Human trafficking—slave labor or forced prostitution—is a growing problem because of the lack of opportunities in Mongolia and the easy transport to Southeast Asia and Eastern Europe on the rail system. I taught a course, for all the high school kids, on immigration policies and human trafficking. My job was to scare the hell out of these kids. I felt that the best way to make them understand was to show them how the world can be a very cold place if you're not prepared. I think I got through to a lot of them. One girl said to me it was the scariest shit she ever heard.

Many young girls in Bulgan got pregnant, just like in my old neighborhoods. But the Mongolian men handled the situation differently from how men back home did. The Mongolians believe that if you have a kid, even if you are only a teenager, you never leave that child. The baby is your lineage, your source of pride. So when teenagers had kids, they embraced the situation. Many of the sixteen-year-old boys I worked with would go home after school to take care of their kids. They'd walk around town showing off their little baby boy or girl. They taught their kids how to do all types of things, like how to say the one or two words they knew in English. These young men were as poor as anyone in the 'hood, but they stayed involved in their kids' lives.

My cousin just had his second baby, before he turned eighteen. My mom was a teenager when she had her first child. My sister got pregnant at fourteen. She fell in love with her boyfriend. She thought he was someone she could be with for the rest of her life. But once she had the baby, he left, and reality dawned on her: Playtime's over.

The dudes in the 'hood walk away because none of them ever had a dad around. Being a single parent is a vicious cycle. If that's all you know, then that's what you follow. My cousin had his first child with someone he thought was the love of his life, this girl he had gone to school with for three years. Then he found that when the baby comes, the relationship's not the same. In the 'hood, men walk away because there's no strong social pressure that says you should be ashamed for walking away.

In Mongolia, they don't have a conventional marriage ceremony, like we do. There, if you live with someone for more than five days, she's your wife. If you have a kid with someone, she's your wife. They see manhood as standing up to your responsibilities by caring for your family and contributing to your community. If you fail to do that, by leaving your wife or your child, they treat you no better than they treat the local drunks. And they treat the local drunks pretty badly. If you're a herder or you're a farmer, you're something in Mongolia. But if you can't be a man, you get no respect.

· · · ·

There is a cult of personality in Mongolia that's built around Genghis Khan. To Mongolians, he was the pinnacle of manhood, the greatest warrior the world has ever known. They worship him for his brute strength, sense of responsibility, decisiveness, and brave heart. Every Mongolian man aspires to be like him. Stores are named after him. Universities are named after him. There's even a vodka named after him; it's goddamn terrible, but it has Genghis Khan's name on it, so the Mongolians think it's the world's best vodka. Parents name their kids after Genghis Khan; his original name was Temüjin, so that is the most common boy's name in Mongolia. If I had ever said one negative word about Genghis Khan, guys would have whupped my ass.

Mongolian men can read. The literacy rate is 90 percent. Their educational philosophy is based on the Russian system, where every child must go to school through the eighth grade and learn the basics. The people of Bulgan City were proud of the fact that you couldn't find anyone there who didn't know how to read. So they know their history. They knew that Genghis Khan would kill every elder in the villages he conquered so that people knew he wasn't one to fuck with. By having sex with the women of the villages he made sure his lineage would be passed on. And he burned the villages to the ground so that people couldn't rise up against him after he conquered them. Modern Mongolians know all this, and they still worship Khan; yet, on the whole, they are not violent. Certainly, if you give a couple of men a bottle of vodka on a Friday night, you might have a street brawl. But otherwise they've figured out what being a good man is all about.

• • • •

The movie *Scarface* always was big in the 'hood. Every dude thought the movie showed how you earned respect: When you had to handle business, you handled it, and you had no regrets. Everyone wanted to be like Tony Montana. A blue-collar job—nine-to-five—was for the birds. You knew you weren't going to be driving a nice car if you were pushing the mail and just doing an honest day's work. People wanted to have the nice clothes and the nice cars, and you got that only by making quick money, only by pushing weight. That's what dudes admired. You either sold drugs, you had a mean jump shot, or you hustled some other way. Legitimacy wasn't cool. That's some shit for the sucker.

In the 'hood, jail is a badge of honor. That's the craziest shit I've ever heard, to wake up one day saying, "I'm going to go to jail to get some street cred." I can promise you the people in jail serving twenty-five to life would be the first to tell you they wish they'd never done it that way. My uncle did twelve years in a state prison that was considered one of the worst in this country. And he hated every moment of it, man. My little cousin, a twelve-year-old, would say, "When I'm eighteen, I'm going to go to prison too, so I get the status like he has." My uncle set him straight right away. "Fuck that," he told my cousin. "You want to have to go to a shower every day watching your back?"

The success I had is what any parent would want for their kid.

What parent says, "I want my kid to live a life full of risk"? That's what you get as a drug dealer or a gangster. You end up dead or you end up in a jail, or forty years from now, when you're sixty years old, you end up wishing you could have done your life a different way.

But as soon as I got out of the 'hood, my cousins had no respect for me. They would say, "Oh, you're reading now. Your language is proper. You've got goals in life. You're a white boy now. You ain't one of us." When you got an education, you weren't part of the 'hood anymore. You had sold out and become like one of the white boys.

I remember when I was working for John Kerry's presidential campaign, and I heard Barack Obama speak at the Democratic convention. At one point he said that it shouldn't be wrong to want to learn, and that a black kid shouldn't be considered a sellout because he likes to read. I was sitting with a bunch of African-American friends, and we went wild because we had all grown up in the 'hood, where that was the message, that reading was wrong.

Some members of my family were proud that I had gone to college and got an education, but they couldn't understand why I went into the Peace Corps. When I got back home from Mongolia, I wanted to tell everybody about the world, about all the great things I had seen. But people didn't care, especially in the 'hood. My family members criticized me. They said, "You just paid for four years of college. Who goes off and works for free after paying for college? We all got to work and bust our ass, and yet you could just go globe-trot around the world." They couldn't understand that money wasn't my primary objective. It ended up being a huge sticking point, so I just kept my experience to myself.

---

# HEART OF A BEGINNER

**ANDRE TIPPETT**

A LOT OF PEOPLE used to think I was a black belt just because I was a professional athlete, that somebody gave me the black belt as some kind of honor. I'm no goddamn honorary black belt. I'm a bona fide black belt who did it on the floor. I got into the NFL Hall of Fame because of karate, not the other way around.

Karate is more than just punching and kicking and knocking somebody out if he steps on your feet. Karate allows you to find out about yourself. Just when you think you can't go anymore, you discover something deep inside that will push you further.

A core idea of martial arts is something called "beginner's mind." I've been doing karate for over thirty years now, but I'm still a beginner. You should never think your ranking is so high that there's nothing more for you to learn. If you do get to that point, you should leave. You should stop training. You should find something else to do with your life. No matter how high your ranking, you always want to keep a beginner's mind. If you do that, there's nothing that you can't achieve in martial arts and through your training.

Having a beginner's mind means that you're open to new ideas. No matter how good you are, no matter how strong and fast you get, no matter how good people tell you that you are, you have to want to continue to train and to get better. You have to have the eagerness—and you can't let preconceptions come into your thought process. Those are the keys to being an athlete and a martial artist.

In the NFL, I assumed every year that every linebacker the Patriots drafted could take my job. So I adopted the white-belt mentality—*shoshin*—heart of a beginner. At each training camp, I went at it as hard as I could. Once the season began, I went hard in games, and I went hard in practice. There were times in practices when guys would look at me as if to say, why are you going so hard? Well, I was practicing the way I planned to play on Sunday. That concept—beginner's mind—followed me through my twelve-year career.

• • • •

Right after I was born, in Alabama, my mom left and went north to establish herself and get a job. During that time—the '50s and '60s—families were leaving the South and going to Chicago, Detroit, New Jersey, New York, California. My clan—my mom's friends and girlfriends who graduated from high school and then decided to get out of Birmingham so they could provide better lives for their kids—chose New Jersey. I grew up with my grandmother in Alabama until I was seven and my sister was six. That's when Mom sent for my sister and me. By that time she had four younger children, too.

My dad was never part of my life. My mom showed me how to be a man. She taught me right from wrong, taught me life skills, how to cook, wash, and to be responsible, be accountable. She was very serious about it, and it has paid off for me. Growing up in Newark was tough; we went without a lot, but I never let that be a hindrance to me. I knew that we lacked certain things that other people did have, but we got by. There was a lot of love in the house, and there was always something to eat. We didn't have fabulous meals, but we seldom went without one.

Being the oldest of my brothers and sisters, I was forced to become mature and responsible at an early age. I was a loner, inquisitive, but also the boy who had to be a man. Even at seven years old, I'd do the laundry at the Laundromat down the block. I would count out the money, put the whites in one pillowcase, colors in another pillowcase, and bring them back clean and folded.

I was always big for my age, so guys were trying me all the time— warranted, unwarranted, just all the time. Mom got after me to stop running in the house every time I got chased home from school. One time she met me at the top of our steps when she saw me running away from a fight. She said, "Andre, you turn around. You're going to fight them. You're not going to keep getting chased home." I dove off the top of the steps onto those guys. That was the end of me getting chased home.

. . . .

There was a karate school in my neighborhood. I always wanted to go in, but Mom would never give me the money. I didn't realize she couldn't afford the twenty-five dollars a month it cost for lessons, not if she wanted to feed us and put clothes on our backs. Finally, when I was eleven, I learned that the Boys & Girls Club was holding karate classes. That's where it all started for me. I learned a lot about self-defense, and I competed in a lot of tournaments—in New York and New Jersey—from about '73 until '78. Even though I started just to protect myself, I learned to love martial arts. Mom gave me the discipline, but karate gave me more structure. It gave me something to look forward to. It was something that I could call my own—I was the only one in my family who did karate.

I didn't start playing football until high school. I actually got cut my freshman year, so technically I didn't start until my sophomore year. I found a new love, on top of karate, to give me a little bit more structure, more discipline, and more meaning in my life. I went from an individual sport to a team sport where you can't get it done without the other ten guys.

After high school, I got a football scholarship to the University of Iowa. The first thing I did when I got there was to figure out where I was going to practice martial arts. I thought I knew a lot about karate, but really I knew nothing. Iowa was my coming-out party. In Newark, the karate was focused on self-defense. If you attack me, if you touch me, you can forget it: I have you, and I will do what I have to do to protect myself. There was no philosophy behind it, no foundation to what I was doing.

But in Iowa I met this group of martial artists who had roots in Okinawa, Japan. They asked me about my training, and all I knew was my instructor's name. I could demonstrate probably twenty self-defense techniques: standing toe-to-toe, up against a wall, my back to you, disarming someone who had a knife, a gun. But these guys were doing kata—predetermined movements, sort of like what a gymnast does in a floor routine. I'd never seen it before, and I thought, man, why am I missing out?

The training went deeper than just punching and kicking. We got into the mental and the spiritual sides of karate. We would talk about mind, body, and spirit, how you can't have one without the others. Through those four years in Iowa, training with these guys, I realized that there was so much more for me to learn. I had earned a black belt, but I wanted to know what else was out there. It got me hungry. It also caused an important shift in my personality. In Newark, I had to protect myself at all times just to survive, so I developed a mean streak that I never turned off. In Iowa, I realized that I didn't have to be that way all the time, only when it's necessary. I saw how these guys I trained with carried themselves, and it showed me that I didn't always have to be on edge—like I was ready to explode anytime somebody said the wrong thing to me—because I wasn't in Newark anymore, and I didn't plan on being in Newark the rest of my life. I'm living in the suburbs now, and I can't go to the grocery store looking like I might hurt you if you grab that loaf of bread before I get it.

When the New England Patriots drafted me, in 1982, I immediately started looking around for a dojo, a karate studio, where I could train, just as I did when I got to Iowa. I found the Okinawan Karate Club right near the stadium. I've been a member there for twenty-seven years now. When I was playing, I would do kata on Friday nights to mentally prepare for a game. In our karate system, we have nine katas, from a white-belt kata all the way up to the highest black-belt kata. When you do kata, you should be visualizing that you're in a fight. I would visualize certain movements, certain attacks and counters. It would get me geared up for a game, prepare me for battle.

· · · ·

In karate, all your answers are on the floor. You can't get them by reading a book or watching a video; they're on the floor. You step on the floor, and you work it out, and you'll find the answers. We want to solve our problems through intellect or by pointing a finger at someone else, but none of that works.

To become a good karate student, to make your technique better, you have to train harder, punch harder, do kicks harder, work on making your hands faster, and develop timing and balance. You can do that only by sweating on the floor and pushing yourself and motivating yourself to go harder. You can't just go through the motions. You can't pace yourself. You have to go all out when you're on the floor, and the more you do it, the better you're going to become.

The answers are on the football field, too. You have to practice the way you plan on playing. You can't take plays off. You can't wish yourself good. You have to do the off-season running, lifting, taking care of your body, and then you have to maintain that during the season. You work hard during the week. You prepare. You push your teammates. You push yourself. Come game time on Sunday, it should be easy for you. There are not going to be any surprises.

I didn't really take advantage of the connection between martial arts and football until I got into the NFL. Unlike high school and college, where just being an athlete and being quick was enough, in the NFL there was an Andre Tippett on every team—a guy who was my physical equal. So I had to have something that would set me apart and allow me to beat these guys. During the 1983 season—my second in the league and first as a permanent starter—I made it clear that I was different from all the other linebackers in the NFL. And it was because I began to understand how much my karate training could help me in football.

To get to the quarterback, to put pressure on him or get him on the ground, I had to come up with a lot of different ways to pass rush. I was able to manipulate linemen, to defend myself and knock their hands off me, in ways I had been practicing almost my whole life. I had hand speed. I knew about leverage. I knew when to release a running back who was trying to block me and when to hand punch him. These were all just natural reactions to defend myself. Karate is a combat sport, and so is football. It's either me beating you or you beating me, and I'm not going to let you beat me. I've got to figure out how to get the advantage in every situation.

My mental approach to football also came directly from my karate teachers. They taught me to refuse to quit. If you knocked me down seven times, I would get up seven times. I would just wear you out. I would keep going. I wouldn't stop. I did it in workouts. I did it in testing situations. You really do surprise yourself. You knock out ten punches, ten blocks. You can't go anymore. Sensei is yelling, "One more time!" Boom, boom, and you just keep doing it. And over a period of time, years and years of doing that, it becomes habit. You don't let anybody see your fear; you don't let them see you sweat it out. All they see is an indomitable spirit. You put that on somebody, and it works, in karate and on the football field.

# RESOLUTION

JOSEPH LEVENS

COMING HOME VERY LATE from work one night, I see that my car is the only one remaining in the dark train-station parking lot. It's parked by a line of white pines in the back. A girl is standing beside the trees, beside my car, with her arms crossed and her feet shifting. She has no coat on—in November, in New York. We look at each other: I do not know her, and she does not know me. I get in my car and drive home.

It is the middle of a workday in Midtown, and I'm off to another meeting in another office, walking along another city sidewalk. A car hits the back of an idling cab, and the cab careens into the knees of another businessman, knocking him down. I look at the man: He cannot get up. I continue walking.

The morning of September 11, 2001, I am working from home on

Long Island, twenty miles from Manhattan. News footage shows plumes of smoke moving east with the wind. I shut my window.

The street peddler outside my new office, in Chelsea, wants only twenty-five cents for a banana. I had worked for almost ten years in Times Square, where, inside a warm deli, I was paying fifty cents for the same. Now this man, who feels the cold all winter and rolls his cart back and forth each day, gets only half that price.

Over the years, one of my staff has become one of my best friends. But the company is doing badly now, and jobs are being sent to India. He is going to be let go. I knew this several months in advance. On the day he is dismissed, it is a shock to him.

Getting off the train on my way home, on yet another day, I see a group of bored teenagers hanging about the station. "How was work today, mister?" they ask Gerry, a financial broker who is always a few steps ahead of me. Day after day, he positions himself perfectly between the train door and the up-and-over stairs. "Fine," he says and keeps walking. "Howdy, ma'am," the boys say to a businesswoman. I have seen her before; I don't know her name or where she works, only that she likes to get up from her seat well before the train pulls in, and that, in all likelihood, blue is her favorite color. "Did you have a good day today, sir?" the kids ask me. "No. How was your day?" I say. "Excellent," says one boy. "Awesome," says another.

It's New Year's Eve, and I feel as though my one big resolution should be to work on my disposition, to be nicer and more amenable, considerate, honest, sensitive, forgiving, to look on the brighter side. I decide to go ahead with this plan, and I have another drink.

· · · ·

One January morning, a newspaper strews all over the platform at Penn Station. I see the man who tossed it onto the cement as he got off the train. I approach him and point out the mess he's made. He pushes me, and my head hits that of a woman behind me. I see blood form above her right eye. "You're bleeding," I say. "Shit," she says.

At work, I'm asked if I could give the water cooler man a hand and replace the empty bottle in the coffee room; his back is bad. I help him, and now my back is bad.

On my way home, an old lady standing beside a subway turn-stile fumbles with the contents of her pocketbook. She can't find her MetroCard. Her cane dangles under her arm, her glasses are slipping off her face, her head shakes nervously back and forth. I swipe my card in the machine and tell her to walk through. "You go, dear," she says. "I will find it." I tell her it is all right, to go on. As we debate, a kid runs through the gate.

An exciting new internal job opportunity is posted at work. I mention it to a friend of mine in another department, and she says she really would like that position. I tell her to apply, that I don't want to compete with her. She applies, gets an interview, has dinner with the director, and then an offer. But she turns it down. Soon after, the post is pulled because of strategic changes in company initiatives.

One day in the spring, the 5:38 into the suburbs collides with a vehicle on the tracks. There is likely a fatality, the conductor announces over the speaker. The man in the seat behind me is visibly upset. When I ask why, he says because now they have to shut down the line and bring in the investigators. We will have to be bused, he says. It will take hours for us to get home. I ask him to gather some concern for the person we hit. He says it was probably an idiot, moron suicide. The paper reports the next day that a seventy-two-year-old man on his way home from a final radiation treatment had turned onto the tracks and parked there.

I pay for lunch with colleagues one Friday, and in the afternoon find that all those who do not work in support roles, as I do, will be getting bonuses. Still, I do not expense the meal. It will come out of my own pocket, the pocket of a pair of trousers on a man who is and evermore will be happy, happy, happy with himself.

# The Knight's Prayer
*Robert Pinsky*

He prayed in silence.

Even in his personal extreme
Of woe and dread, which was neither
Heroic nor intolerable but sufficiently
Woeful and dreadful, he would not waver
From that discipline.

In his vanity as severely
Logical as a clever adolescent, he found
All vocal terms of sanctity impertinent.

He also rejected gestures: the stagey pose
Of the figure in armor on one knee,
Hands and brow resting on the cruciform hilt
Of a still-scabbarded weapon.
The words and the pose contradicted
Themselves, their conventionality made them
Symbols of worldly attachment.

Therefore in his own prayers he strove
For intimacy, a near-absence of petition.
In his pride he began to abjure even
The request for the strength to ask nothing.

He prayed for steadfastness. In the exploits
He most envied, heroes of old
Endured hardship and ordeals. Worldly
Attachment was their assigned
Burden of imperfection:
Bearing it was their mission.

*Lest these prayers be*
*For weariness of life, not love of Thee,*
He had read: a standard he admired
Not in the name of love
But for its stringency: the gauntlet
Of chainmail not folded
On the breviary, but brandished,
Able for the task

Then, that abrupt personal extreme
Of woe and dread, neither
Heroic nor intolerable: a cause
To fear the silence.
The soul stammering to itself.

It was not "In fear of the Lord
Is the beginning of wisdom."

But in fear a new
Model for worldly attachment:

It was like the birth
Of an infant: the father, in sudden
Overthrow, turning from indifference
To absolute care, a ferocity
Of petition dwarfing desire—
All vows abrogated, all discipline
Undone, all of life flowing at once
Toward the new, incompetent soul.

# CONTRIBUTORS

## KEITH ACKERS

KEITH ACKERS is a recovering television producer trying harder than ever to nurture his more thoughtful inner English major. Ackers has held management positions at a national network show and several local news affiliates, and currently he is supervising traffic reporting for television clients across the country. His best creative validation came when his daughter recently told him he makes up really good bedtime stories. He says that as far as he can tell, the kid has not yet learned how to lie. Ackers lives with his wife and two children outside Philadelphia.

## AMIN AHMAD

AMIN AHMAD grew up in India, trained as an architect at the Massachusetts Institute of Technology, and never has adjusted to the cold of Boston. His writing bridges the gap between the colonial mansions of his childhood and the creaky, wood-framed house in which he now lives.

## STEVE ALMOND

STEVE ALMOND has authored the essay collection *(Not That You Asked) Rants, Exploits, and Obsessions,* the short story collections *The Evil B.B. Chow* and *My Life in Heavy Metal,* and the nonfiction book *Candyfreak: A Journey through the Chocolate Underbelly of America.* He also is the coauthor (with Julianna Baggott) of the novel *Which Brings Me to You.* Almond was a contributing writer to Alarm Clock Theatre Company's Elliot Norton Award–winning play *P.S. Page Me Later,* based on selections from *Found Magazine.*

## NORM APPEL

NORM APPEL graduated from the Wharton School of Finance in 1958 and then embarked on a Wall Street career that lasted from 1959 until his retirement in 1976. At that point he became a full-time parent for 50 percent of his time and a model and sometime actor for the other 50 percent. After his oldest son, David, passed away in 1993, he returned to a more active role in some of his manufacturing investments. He completely retired from business in 2004 and now spends his time modeling and going on auditions.

## CURTIS B.

CURTIS B. grew up in an East Coast inner city and then went to high school in a predominantly white, upper-class suburb. After college, he served in the Peace Corps, teaching life skills and English to children in Mongolia.

## LARRY BEAN

LARRY BEAN has been an editor of magazines, newspapers, and books. Most recently he was the editor in chief of *Robb Report* magazine. He lives in Massachusetts with his wife and their son and daughter.

## JOE D'ARRIGO

JOE D'ARRIGO established an insurance business when he was twenty-nine and later created an employee benefits advisory firm in Boston. He sold that company to a major insurance company and then became a business-plan consultant. D'Arrigo now is a principal and adviser to one of those companies for which he consulted. Although he loves the work he does, if you asked him where he is most at home, D'Arrigo, who has sailed 25,000 miles in the last seven years, would say, "Barefoot on the deck of a sailboat offshore."

## BRUCE ELLMAN

BRUCE ELLMAN is a clinical psychologist and organizational consultant in Los Angeles. A father of three, Ellman is a graduate of Brown University, and he holds an MBA from Yale University and a doctorate in clinical psychology from Pepperdine University.

## RICARDO FEDERICO

RICARDO (RIC) FEDERICO works, writes, and lives in southern Kentucky with his incredibly supportive wife and three teenage children. When he isn't experimenting with essays, short stories, or a novel, Federico often can be found at the driveway basketball hoop or on a walking trail. Once a week he usually manages to have lunch with his father, the guy who taught him so much about doing whatever it takes.

## PAUL FURTAW

PAUL FURTAW is a husband, father, brother, and son, as well as a licensed psychologist. In his professional practice, he attends to the well-being of college students and health care practitioners-in-training while also consulting to higher education, health care, and human service organizations. He remains a proponent of the "talking cure," while at the same time he looks forward to the day when advances in pharmaceutical and biomedical research will allow us all to experience the aging process with our faculties, our memories, and our ties to our loved ones largely intact.

## ROLF GATES

ROLF GATES is the author of *Meditations from the Mat: Daily Reflections on the Path of Yoga*. He conducts Vinyasa intensives and teacher trainings throughout the United States and abroad. A former U.S. Army Airborne Ranger, emergency medical technician, and addictions counselor, Gates has an eclectic background that informs his practice and his teachings. Gates was born in Manhattan and grew up in the Boston area as a marathon runner, long-distance cyclist, and champion wrestler. He now lives in Santa Cruz, California, with his wife, Mariam, and their two children.

## Kent George

Kent George is an actor, writer, and filmmaker living with his wife and two children in Los Angeles. As an actor he has appeared in numerous theater, television, and film projects over the past twenty years. He is a longtime company member of Circus Theatricals in Los Angeles, and he has presented two original plays at the Powerhouse Theater in Santa Monica. In 2006, George wrote and produced the semiautobiographical feature film *Puff, Puff, Pass*. He currently is editing a feature-length documentary titled *Inside the Box*, which is about Circus Theatricals and the lives of theater actors in Los Angeles.

## Regie O'Hare Gibson

Regie O'Hare Gibson is a poet, songwriter, author, workshop facilitator, and educator. His work appears in the New Line Cinema film *Love Jones*, which is based largely on events in his life. His poem "Brother to the Night (A Blues for Nina)" is on the movie's sound track and is performed by the film's star, Larenz Tate. In the film, Gibson performs "Hey Nappy Head" with percussionist and composer Kahil El'Zabar, who arranged the score for the theatrical version of *The Lion King*.

## Perry Glasser

Perry Glasser is the author of *Dangerous Places*, a collection of short fiction that received the 2008 G.S. Sharat Chandra Prize from BkMk Press at the University of Missouri–Kansas City. He has published two prior collections of short fiction, *Suspicious Origins* and *Singing on the Titanic*. A native of Brooklyn, Glasser taught writing and literature at Drake University in Iowa and was a professor of English at Bradford College in Massachusetts. Since 2003, Glasser has been the coordinator of the Professional Writing Program at Salem State College in Massachusetts.

## Stuart Horwitz

Stuart Horwitz is the founder of Book Architecture, a manuscript assistance firm that helps writers prepare their work for presentation to publishing houses. Horwitz is a published poet and is the front man for the poetry/punk-funk band Art Don't Pay. He holds two master's degrees, one from New York University, in religious studies and literature, and one from Harvard University, in East Asian studies. He has been married for twelve years and is the father of one amazing kid.

## JAMES HOUGHTON

JAMES HOUGHTON has had a varied career as an investment banker in New York and London, a business manager for Corning Inc., and a partner in the early-stage venture capital firm founded by *The Good Men Project* coeditor Tom Matlack. He lives in Boston with his wife and their two children.

## MICHAEL KAMBER

MICHAEL KAMBER is a photojournalist who has covered wars throughout the world. He has been nominated for three Pulitzer Prizes, twice for photography and once for writing. His current home base is the Baghdad bureau of the *New York Times*.

## STEPHEN KARL KLOTZ

STEPHEN KARL KLOTZ is a native of Williamsport, Pennsylvania, which, as the home of Little League Baseball, is a great father-child destination. Klotz now lives in York, Pennsylvania. He has two grown sons who are married and living away from home, but he frequently talks and visits with them. Klotz's retired racing greyhound, Buck, keeps him company at home, and they enjoy walking together, whether around the neighborhood or on a nearby trail. Klotz teaches communication techniques to people who care for older persons with dementia. He is working on both nonfiction and fiction projects.

## CHRISTOPHER KOEHLER

CHRISTOPHER KOEHLER realized while writing his dissertation in an obscure and specious corner of cultural studies that, though he lived to write, academic writing sucked the life out of his prose. So he bailed on academe shortly after entering it. His nonfiction and fiction both focus on the history of science and medicine. When he's not parenting, writing, or rowing, he works as an editorial assistant for a scientific journal and as a freelance editor. He lives in Northern California with his husband and son.

## JESSE KORNBLUTH

JESSE KORNBLUTH is a New York–based journalist and editor of the cultural concierge service (books, music, movies) HeadButler.com. He has been a contributing editor for *Vanity Fair* and *New York*, and a contributor to the *New Yorker*, the *New York Times*, and other publications. In 1996, he cofounded Bookreporter.com. From 1997 to 2002, he was editorial director of America Online. His books include *Highly Confident:*

*The Crime and Punishment of Michael Milken, Airborne: The Triumph and Struggle of Michael Jordan,* and *Pre-Pop Warhol.*

## CHARLIE LEDUFF

CHARLIE LEDUFF is the author of *US Guys: The True and Twisted Mind of the American Man.* In addition to being a writer, he also is a filmmaker and a multimedia reporter for the *Detroit News.* He is a former national correspondent for the *New York Times.* He covered the war in Iraq, crossed the desert with a group of migrant Mexicans, and worked inside a North Carolina slaughterhouse as part of the *Times'* series "How Race Is Lived in America," which was awarded the 2001 Pulitzer Prize for National Reporting.

## JOSEPH LEVENS

JOSEPH LEVENS is the editor of the *Summerset Review.* His work, primarily fiction, has appeared in the *Florida Review* (2007 Editors' Award winner), *AGNI, New Orleans Review, Swink, Other Voices, Meridian, Sou'wester,* and other places. He has completed a collection of stories and, like everyone else, is at work on a novel.

## TOM MATLACK

TOM MATLACK is an eighth-generation descendant of Timothy Matlack, the man who was the scribe for the Declaration of Independence. Matlack also is a second-generation descendant of Pearl Buck, the first American woman to receive the Nobel Prize for Literature. He worked on Wall Street, was CFO of a major media company, and started his own venture capital firm before turning to writing full time. He lives in Boston with his wife and three children.

## JULIO MEDINA

JULIO MEDINA served twelve years in prison for gang-related crimes. He emerged a changed man, dedicated to helping other inmates make the transition, once they were released from prison, from criminals to good men and good fathers. His organization, Exodus Transitional Community, has served more than 3,000 men and women and has become one of the country's most successful reentry programs.

## John Oliver

JOHN OLIVER grew up in a working-class family in Detroit, graduated from West Point, and served in the 82nd Airborne Division during the first Gulf War. Oliver now lives in Richmond, Virginia, with his wife and three children.

## Robert Pinsky

ROBERT PINSKY was named the poet laureate of the United States in 1997. He now lives in Newton Corner, Massachusetts, and teaches in the graduate writing program at Boston University. As the U.S. poet laureate, Pinsky founded the Favorite Poem Project, in which thousands of Americans of varying backgrounds and ages and from every state share their favorite poems. Pinsky guest-starred in a 2002 episode of *The Simpsons* and appeared on *The Colbert Report* in 2007, as the judge of a Meta-Free-Phor-All between Stephen Colbert and Sean Penn.

## Joel Schwartzberg

JOEL SCHWARTZBERG is the author of *The 40-Year-Old Version: Humoirs of a Divorced Dad*. Schwartzberg's essays have been published in *Newsweek*, the *New York Times Magazine*, the *New York Daily News*, *New Jersey Monthly*, and other publications throughout the United States and Canada. A former online executive with Nickelodeon and Time Inc., Schwartzberg is currently the director of new media for a PBS broadcast news magazine. He lives in Montclair, New Jersey, with his wife and—on Saturdays—his three kids.

## John Sheehy

JOHN SHEEHY is a professor of writing and literature at Marlboro College in Vermont. He holds an MA and a PhD from the University of Washington. Sheehy grew up in Montana, the grandson of Irish immigrants who came to Montana to mine copper in Butte. Although Con, his Irish grandfather, contracted lung disease in the mines and died before Sheehy was born, Con and the rest of the Butte Irish left a large impact on their descendants.

## Mark St. Amant

MARK ST. AMANT is an author and award-winning advertising writer whose first book, *Committed: Confessions of a Fantasy Football Junkie*, is the top-selling fantasy football book of all time. His second book, *Just Kick It: Tales of an Underdog, Over-Age, Out-of-Place Semi-Pro Football Player*, chronicled St. Amant's unforgettable season kicking for an inner-city Boston semipro team. He was the first fantasy sports writer for NYTimes.com's "Fifth Down" NFL blog, and writes a popular weekly column, "Fantasy Man-Crush Index," for NBC Sports' Rotoworld.com.

## ANDRE TIPPETT

ANDRE TIPPETT is an NFL Hall of Fame linebacker. He was born in Birmingham, Alabama, into a fatherless home, where he had to help raise his younger brother and sisters. He was an all-American at the University of Iowa before being drafted by the New England Patriots in 1982. Tippett is a Godan/fifth-degree black belt with a Shihan (Master Instructor) license.

## JEFFREY K. WALLACE

JEFFREY K. WALLACE lives in Orange County, California. When he's not reading, writing, parenting, or teaching (at Chapman University), he's busy enjoying his family. Wallace's essays have appeared in the *Los Angeles Times*, *Family Circle* magazine, the *Orange County Register*, *Toastmaster International*, and the anthology *I Wanna Be Sedated: 30 Writers on Parenting Teenagers*.

## CARY WONG

CARY WONG received his MFA in playwriting from Columbia University. He was a Van Lier Playwriting Fellow at Manhattan Theatre Club. His MTC-commissioned play, *Mirrors Remembered*, was produced at New York Stage and Film. His plays have had readings at the Public Theater, MTC, Queens Theatre in the Park, Mark Taper Forum, and East West Players. Wong also is a columnist and reviewer for the online magazine *Film Score Monthly*.

## BEN WOODBECK

BEN WOODBECK has been a wilderness instructor for fifteen years, logging more than 1,500 days leading expeditions with wayward youths to remote locations in North America. Woodbeck has climbed peaks in North America, South America, and Asia, paddled great distances on long rivers, run a few 100-mile races, found ways to extend adolescence, and tried to write about it. He reads, writes, runs, and lives in rural Colorado and is proud of his Midwestern roots.

# ACKNOWLEDGMENTS

THE GOOD MEN PROJECT would not have happened without the extraordinary effort, wise counsel, and patient support of many good men and women. The list is long, and we are grateful to you all—even if we neglected to name you here. We have been both humbled and inspired by the passion and dedication and candor of all who have given their time and talent to this endeavor.

First and foremost, we would like to acknowledge the core members of *The Good Men Project*'s production team, the people who have been involved since the early days and those who have joined along the way, all of whose professional expertise and advice have made the final product infinitely better. Thank you especially to Cathy Vaughan, our peerless project administrator; Stephen Sheffield, whose photographs inspired our Web site and now grace the book; Joey Kolchinsky and his team at OneVision Resources for designing and managing the Web site that launched it all; Gina Caruso, our creative events planner and coordinator; Mark St. Amant, for both the engaging essay he contributed to the anthology and his advertising expertise; Andrea Lenig, for all her help with advertising and promotion; Matt Gannon, whose compelling documentary film has brought *The Good Men Project* to life; Richard Poulin, AJ Mapes, and Michael Bebout of Poulin + Morris, for their thoughtful and comprehensive approach to designing the book; Brian Pass of Sheppard Mullin, for his pro bono legal counsel; Brent O'Connor and John Gates, for all their help and guidance with public relations; Jamie Kittler and Chris Tambasco of JDJ Resources, for keeping the finances and accounting straight; Nikki Arena, for her amazingly creative ten-second videos promoting the essays; Karen Cakebread, for her painstaking copyediting and proofreading; and Lisa Hickey, our twenty-four-hour-a-day creative visionary, who solved crisis after crisis with an artistic sensibility that touched every aspect of the final product, from the ads and events to our Web presence, the film, and the book.

We also thank all those who have helped guide the book and the project with their thoughtful input and feedback at various stages of the project. Many thanks to Alison Lobron, for her early editing; Ike Williams and Katherine Flynn of Kneerim & Williams, for their early support and willingness to represent us to publishers; Will Schwalbe, for sharing his publishing expertise and providing early critical feedback on the manuscript; Andrew Blauner, for his encouragement and for sharing many of his contacts in the publishing world; Bill Patten, for believing early; Steven Botkin of Men's Resources International, for his perspective on the men's movement; Rick Melvoin of Belmont Hill School, for sharing his wisdom on the education of boys; and especially to Neil Chethik, for his willingness to lend hours of support and guidance based on his own experience publishing a book by a man for men.

In addition, we thank Frank Mundo and Jean Matlack, for their many shouts of enthusiasm from Rockport, Maine; Kerry Matlack, for her close readings and for attempting to keep her dad somewhat in line;

Liz Benedict, for unleashing Tom's torrent of *Good Men*–related columns on the Huffington Post; Chris Castellani and Whitney Scharer at Grub Street, for promoting our project; *Rowing News*, *Maxim*, *Climbing*, and *American Profile*, for running public service announcements about the project; John Warthen, for telling Tom some twenty-five years ago he had writing talent (the jury is still out, though the encouragement in some ways was what started this whole thing); Carlo Rotella, for his example of great writing; Paul Kidwell, for coming up with the Manhood Quiz; and Will Scoggins, who was Tom's original teacher about manhood, whether in boats or on dry land.

We also would not have made it through the process without the dedication and understanding of our wives: Elena Matlack, Connie Coburn, and Michelle Seaton. You sustain us and make us better men every day.

Finally, we want to thank all the contributors to the book, the documentary film, and the Web site. Your stories are what inspired us in the first place, and *The Good Men Project* is for you. Thank you for your courage and candor and for the grace of your lives.

— *James, Larry, and Tom*

This book was set in Brioni and Ziggurat.

BRIONI is a hybrid of calligraphic influences and subtle manipulation of its stroke terminals. Brioni was designed by Nikola Djurek in 2008. He was born in Croatia and studied at the Royal Academy of Art in The Hague. Djurek is founder of Typonine studio for graphic and type design and teaches at the University of Zagreb and Academy of Art in Split.

ZIGGURAT takes its cues from the entire aesthetic of early slab serif (or "Egyptian") metal types, primarily those produced in Great Britain between 1815 and 1840. Ziggurat was designed by Jonathan Hoefler in 2000. His work has been exhibited internationally and is included in the permanent collection of the Cooper-Hewitt National Design Museum (Smithsonian Institution) in New York. In 2002, the Association Typographique Internationale (ATypI) presented Hoefler with its most prestigious award, the Prix Charles Peignot, for outstanding contributions to type design.